RISK MANAGEMENT
Memory Jogger™

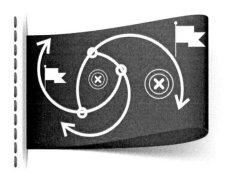

Carl Pritchard, PMP®, PMI-RMP®, EVP
Karen Tate, PMP®, MBA, PMI Fellow

First Edition | GOAL/QPC

MEMORY JOGGER

We remember the tools for you

The Risk Management Memory Jogger™

Development Team:
  Authors: Carl Pritchard, Karen Tate
  Project Management:
    Daniel Griffiths
    Susan Griebel
  Designer: Janet MacCausland

Publication Review Team:
  Mark Anthony, *Premier Risk Solutions*, LLC
  John Bloxham II, *Cameron International*
  Cathy Kenny, *Kaiser Permanente*
  Peter Mihalick, *Total Quality Services*
  John Thaller, *JST Technical Services*, LLC

GOAL/QPC | Memory Jogger
8E Industrial Way, Suite 3, Salem, NH 03079
800.643.4316 or 603.893.1944
service@goalqpc.com
MemoryJogger.org

Printed in the United States of America
ISBN: 978-1-57681-159-7

10 9 8 7 6 5 4 3 2

The Complete How-To Pocket Guide

Statistical Methods Seven Quality Control Tools

Continuous Improvement and Standardization

Managers, Individual, and Improvement Teams

Customer/Supplier Senior Executive Teams

Quality Systems Quality Function Deployment (QFD)

7 Management and Planning (7MP) Tools

Information Systems/Audit Tools

Customer Driven Master Plan

Daily Management

Planning

Cross-Functional Management

STANDARDIZATION

HOW

WHAT

GOAL ALIGNMENT

WHAT

WHO

WHAT

HOW

HORIZONTAL INTEGRATION

TQM Wheel Source:
TQM Master Plan: An Implementation Strategy Research Report, GOAL/QPC

How to Use this Pocket Guide

This pocket guide is designed for you to use as a convenient and quick reference guide. The "*What is it?*" "*Why do it?*" and "*How do I do it?*" format offers you an easy way to navigate through the information in each section.

Use this guide as a reference on the job, or during and after your training, or as part of a self-study program, or to reacquaint yourself with the different types of tools/processes and their uses.

This simple reference is intended to take away some of the fear of complexity associated with risk management for managers, project managers, team members, and executives without a deep background in risk.

What do the different positions of runners mean?

Getting Ready—When you see the "getting ready" position of the runner, expect a brief description of the tool's purpose of the step or task, or the purpose of using a tool and its benefits.

Cruising—When you see this runner, expect to find guidelines and interpretation tips. This is the action phase that provides you with step-by-step instructions and helpful formulas.

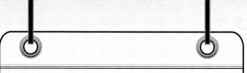 **Finishing the Course**—When you see this runner, expect to see the result of a task/step or a tool in its final form.

To Find a Term

Use the **Glossary** in the back of the book to find industry terms and definitions.

To Find the Start of Each Chapter

Look for the solid bar at the bottom of the page. At the start of each chapter, there is also a Risk Road Map that shows the five steps in the risk management process described in this book.

To Find the Case Study

Go to Appendix A. The case study (Appendix A) follows an organization as it implements a merger with a competitor.

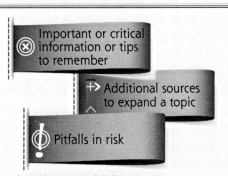

⊗ Important or critical information or tips to remember

⊹ Additional sources to expand a topic

◑ Pitfalls in risk

To Find Tips and Pitfalls

Look for these tags for insights on how best to leverage the risk process or how to avoid many of the common pitfalls associated with process implementation.

Additional Pocket Guide References

GOAL/QPC Memory Joggers are referenced in this pocket guide, and are shown as acronyms.

The Memory Jogger™ 2 ....MJ2
The Creativity Tools Memory Jogger™ ....CTMJ
The Project Management Memory Jogger™ 2nd Ed. PMMJ2

Contents

Preface

RISK MANAGEMENT

is the fine art of dealing with the challenges of what could happen in a simple, orderly fashion. The guidance in this book is not designed to help you avoid all risks or even to bring them all to light. It is instead a chance for you to clarify how to predict as many risks as practicable and to deal with those that need to be dealt with.

The essence of risk management is to be slightly clairvoyant, based on what you already know and how you've managed it in the past. It's coupled with finding out what others know and have managed in order to create the broadest possible understanding of risks and how to cope with them.

— Carl Pritchard, PMP®, PMI-RMP®, EVP

— Karen Tate, PMP®, MBA, PMI Fellow

Establish
Tolerances,
Thresholds
and Triggers

Risk
Management
Plan Cycle

Define
Probability
and Impact

About this Book

The Risk Management Memory Jogger™ (RMMJ) was written by Carl Pritchard, PMP®, PMI-RMP®, EVP and Karen Tate, PMP®, MBA, PMI Fellow to serve as a fundamental resource for those who need guidance on risk management from an individual, project or organizational perspective.

Risk management has evolved in recent years as a business imperative. As with the other books in the Memory Jogger series, the RMMJ provides a solid foundation to improve the success of your organization.

This pocket guide features a comprehensive look at the process of risk management and is aligned with both A Guide to the Project Management Body of Knowledge (A PMBOK® Guide), as well as with ISO 31000: Risk Management: Principles and Guidelines. The RMMJ breaks down the risk management process by first examining the infrastructure of a good risk management practice, and then walking through the processes of risk management, including planning, identification, analysis, response development and control.

The RMMJ is rich with tools that can be applied in virtually any environment. But while there are a host of tools, not all are applicable in every situation, and not all are required or needed for every effort.

While this guide promotes a process, every organization's risk management process will vary. The key is to create a degree of consistency and to institutionalize the practices so that risk becomes part and parcel of regular performance within the organization.

Introduction

This pocket guide includes tools and techniques that range from classics of the practice to the latest, newest approaches. This book is closely aligned with the *A Guide to the Project Management Body of Knowledge*, as well as with ISO 31000: *Risk Management – Principles and Guidelines*.

A PMBOK® *Guide* is the global standard for project management published by the Project Management Institute (PMI). PMI is the largest not-for-profit membership association for the project management profession. PMI's resources and research empower more than 700,000 members, credential holders and volunteers in nearly every country in the world to enhance their careers, improve their organizations' success and further mature the profession. **pmi.org**

ISO, the International Organization for Standardization, is a global organization promoting international standards for business, government and society. ISO 31000 establishes processes that can readily be tailored for different organizations based on their needs and structure.

The differences in an organization's needs are as varied as the organizations themselves. The risk practices they embrace will need to be adapted to fit their specific needs. The basic processes of risk management can still be applied whether organizations are virtual or co-located, traditional or agile, hierarchical or lean. The key is to ensure that processes and terminology are consistently established and applied. This pocket guide offers a wealth of options to choose from in establishing these processes.

Leadership Summary

Why is risk management important?

Risk management…

- identifies the bad and good things that may affect project and organizational success.
- creates early warning systems.
- provides focus on what to deal with first.
- generates strategies to align risks with organizational culture.
- solves problems before they happen.
- creates best practices for the future.

What's involved in the risk management process?

- The organization sets its parameters for what's worth worrying about and what's not.
- The key stakeholders identify threats and opportunities, clarifying the categories, causes and effects.
- The risks are evaluated for their individual impact and their impact on the organization as a whole, through subjective and objective criteria, using a variety of tools.
- Responses are created for the high-probability and high-impact risks, while the lower probability and impact risks are acknowledged and accepted.
- The success and failure of the strategies are evaluated, best practices are documented, and the cycle begins anew.

Who has risk accountability?

Person or group	is accountable for...
Senior Management	Establishing the degrees to which the organization must worry about threats or must pursue opportunities.
	Creating reserves of time and money to ensure opportunities for overall success.
Functional Manager	Establishing the degrees to which the functional organization will accept or reject threats and opportunities.
	Affording a functional perspective on risks in a particular situation, especially technical risks.
	Reviewing the risk exposure for decision-making.
Project Sponsor	Establishing the degrees to which the risks of a project will be be consistently tolerated or avoided.
	Supporting project managers in their efforts to create viable response strategies for risks.
	Validating estimates and approving risk response strategies.
Project Manager	Shepherding the organization and the project team through the entire risk process on an iterative basis.
	Creating a team culture that supports the right level of concern for threats and encouragement for opportunities.

Person or group	is accountable for...
Project Manager	Making sure the risk analyses are not static, but evolving as the project or effort evolves.
Project Teams	Identifying and analyzing risks based on the team's experience, attitudes and norms.
	Alerting the team as risk triggers are observed.
	Implementing specific risk strategies demanded by the situation or selected by the team.
Project Customer	Clarifying the culture and environment in which the risks may transpire.
	Identifying and analyzing risks that are specific to the team's conditions/situations.
Vendors and Others	Conducting risk identification and analysis based on their culture and environment and their understanding of stakeholder tolerances, and providing that information to the appropriate parties within the organization.
	Providing support documentation and other collateral information that clarifies the settings in which risks may involve stakeholders.
Risk Owner	Tracking individual risks and their current probabilities/impacts, as well as following through on strategy implementation.

QUIZ Do You *Really* Know Risk Management?

We all know we have risks. Knowing isn't the same as managing. This book begins with an understanding that you have risks and they need to be managed. It's a powerful, simple set of tools to put you on the path to managing your risks more consistently, more effectively and more proactively than you have in the past. It's your opportunity for planned clairvoyance. *Answers are on the last page of this book.*

1. Risk management is designed to:
   a) Solve all risks
   b) Correct problems as they happen, minimizing impact
   c) Resolve major problems proactively
   d) Create an environment where risks are dealt with appropriately

2. Planning for risk management is focused on:
   a) Identifying risks
   b) Creating a risk culture
   c) Analyzing risks for probability and impact
   d) Choosing risk responses

3. Every risk consists of three key elements. They are:
   a) Event, probability and impact
   b) Strategy, approach and event
   c) Event, uncertainty and probability
   d) Time, cost and requirements

4. One sign of a poor risk management culture is:
   a) Team members talking about risk at every meeting
   b) Customers participating in the risk process
   c) Management being unpredictable in its response to individual concerns
   d) Proactive attitudes about the future

5. The risk management plan should include:
  a) List of all identified risks
  b) Language of risk management as it will be used on the effort
  c) Details on the strategies to be deployed
  d) All of the above

6. Identifying points beyond which an organization will not go is the identification of:
  a) Tolerance
  b) Threshold
  c) Triggers
  d) All of the above

7. A trigger is best defined as:
  a) Indication that a risk has passed
  b) Indication that a risk is happening or imminent
  c) Point beyond which an organization will not go
  d) Point at which organizational behavior should change

8. Probability is the:
  a) Condition of total uncertainty
  b) Degree to which a risk will affect the organization
  c) Likelihood of the occurrence of a risk event
  d) The likelihood of the occurrence of a risk event coupled with the degree of impact

9. In identifying risks, the goal is to:
  a) Identify all risks
  b) Identify most risks
  c) Identify as many risks as practicable
  d) Identify the big risks

10. Monte Carlo analysis generates:
  a) A list of specific risk events
  b) A chart of likely risk events
  c) A chart of the distribution of possible outcomes
  d) A ranking of possible outcomes of specific risk events

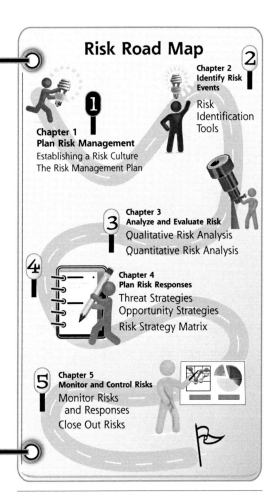

Risk Road Map

Chapter 1
Plan Risk Management
Establishing a Risk Culture
The Risk Management Plan

Chapter 2
Identify Risk Events
Risk Identification Tools

Chapter 3
Analyze and Evaluate Risk
Qualitative Risk Analysis
Quantitative Risk Analysis

Chapter 4
Plan Risk Responses
Threat Strategies
Opportunity Strategies
Risk Strategy Matrix

Chapter 5
Monitor and Control Risks
Monitor Risks and Responses
Close Out Risks

The Risk Management Memory Jogger™ | ©2013 GOAL/QPC

Chapter

ONE

PLAN RISK MANAGEMENT

○ Establishing a Risk Culture

○ The Risk Management Plan

What is it?

Risk is what may happen to you, good or bad, that will influence how your projects, work, and even your lives may turn out. Risk management is the process-driven approach that takes you through the uncertainties of those events.

Why do it?

It's one thing to cope with problems whirling around you, but it's another to actually manage them. Risk management makes dealing with the unpredictable aspects of work more predictable. It's a matter of clarifying what can go wrong (or right), and having a plan to avoid it, live with it, or minimize it.

Establishing a Risk Culture

Every organization, project, household and individual has its own risk culture. It's the processes people use. Risk culture is what you will or will not tolerate. It is also specific terms and language. That's how organizations, individuals and management subgroups define their risk environment and culture.

The Risk Management Process

There are two main foundational elements of a risk culture:

○ **Identify – Assess – Respond – Control**

○ **Terms and definitions**

Terms like "high risk" or "moderate impact" need to be defined. Just as Noah Webster defined American culture with a new dictionary, risk managers need to define a risk culture with a definition of terms. No single way is absolute. But consistency is critical.

 Consistency doesn't mean that every step has to be done every time or every term has to be applied the same way on each project. Sometimes it's fine to omit steps or modify terms for a single effort, as long as there's a documented justification as to why certain steps will be followed at certain times, and why they won't be followed at other times.

Some managers will allow terms to be misused for the sake of expediency. Risks, for example, are future phenomena that have not yet occurred. Issues are risks that have happened. Letting someone get by using the term "issue" for "risk" or "risk" for "issue" can lead to confusion about how concerns are being managed.

The Risk Triad

The most basic definition is that of "risk" itself. Every risk is comprised of three aspects:

Risk Triad

Probability

Impact

Event

- The event that may occur that could affect the objectives of the project or organization

- The likelihood of that event (probability)

- The impact of that event if it comes to pass

An understanding of risk begins with a clear, shared acceptance and understanding of the three aspects so risks can be genuinely managed.

 To identify the impact of a risk, use measurable terms such as time, cost, requirements or customer satisfaction.

How do you weigh risks?

Risk management is the process by which individuals and organizations determine the degrees to which risk may affect them, and what actions are appropriate based on that assessment. Because every individual  has different experiences, different environments and different objectives, risk management is different for everyone. The simple effort of selecting the risks worth focusing on is a key component of risk management, since no two individuals are alike. Without risk management, individuals and organizations are left to deal with impacts only as they happen. It's like getting on a crowded highway without knowing the rules of the road.

How Does Risk Management Help Individuals and Organizations?

Risk management represents the rules of the road for maneuvering through uncertainty

Risk Process	Driving Analogy
Risk Management Planning	Driver education
Risk Culture	Driving on the right, rather than the left
Tolerance	Driver will not drive off the road
Threshold	Within 2' of the edge of the road, driver will correct the path
Trigger	Rumble strips
Risk Identification	Knowing what to watch out for
Risk Analysis	Determining which threats are greatest
Risk Response Planning	Wearing a seat belt
Risk Control	Air bag deployment in an accident

All of the structures of risk management can easily be compared to the structures established by any highway authority. The speed limits, the warning signs, the highway patrol officers, the rumble strips and the lane markings all have their analogies in the risk management process. Without those controls, a drive down the road would have the potential to be pure mayhem. With those controls, the driving society generally functions well. The probability and impact of risk events are reduced, and a degree of normal behavior is maintained.

⊗ ╫ Risk management creates a common set of expectations for those who live within a given risk culture.

Signs that indicate an organization has a poor risk culture.

- [ ] Individuals take risks that can put others or the organization at harm.

- [ ] Individuals are overly paranoid about risks that really aren't that great a concern.

- [ ] Individuals take actions to deal with risks, driving up costs and extending timelines.

- [ ] Management appears unpredictable in its response to individual concerns.

- [ ] Efforts are undertaken without a clear understanding of short- and long-term consequences (and the ripple effect to other parts of the organization).

- [ ] Individuals have reactive attitudes about the future.

- [ ] There is a lack of understanding about risks and the future.

- [ ] There is reliance on "hope" as a strategy.

- [ ] The organization skips or shortchanges risk management because of a perceived lack or time.

- [ ] The organization skips or shortchanges risk management to avoid confrontation or bad news.

- [ ] "Fighting fires" is more common than preventing fires.

- [ ] Individuals who raise concerns about risks are labeled as trouble makers, not team players.

If your organization has a poor risk culture, you can build a more positive attitude toward risk, and avoid the misconception that risk management is merely dealing with the negative things that can happen. By applying step-by-step processes, effective and successful risk management can become the standard.

Key Terms to Know

Before launching into risk management, it's important to understand the basic language of risk.

Key Terms	
Risk 	An occurrence (with a degree of uncertainty) that may happen to influence the objective. It can be positive or negative. A risk consists of the event that may happen, the probability of its occurrence, and the impact if it ultimately comes to pass.
Risk Management Plan	A document outlining the details of the approaches, terms, tolerances, timing, and processes to be managed.
Risk Management Process	A process applied to establish norms for risk, and to identify, analyze, respond to, and learn from risk within a given environment.

Key Terms

Risk Owner . . . . An individual who oversees and is accountable for a given risk event.

Threat . . . . A negative risk event.

Threshold . . . . A way to help identify those risks for which specific responses are needed.

Opportunity . . . . A positive risk event.

Probability . . . . The likelihood that a given risk may occur.

Tolerance . . . . The organizational, project-level or individual limit beyond which risks become wholly unacceptable.

Impact . . . . Realistic worst-case or best-case scenario if the risk event happens

Response . . . . The activity, deliverable, or process by which an individual risk will be managed.

Risk Register . . . . A spreadsheet or document providing information about individual risks and their strategies, including events, probabilities, impacts, responses, owners, and review dates.

Risks exist in an environment of uncertainty. If an event is a sure thing? It's an issue.

Building the Glossary

Adopt terms that make sense in your culture. Consider other sources for terms as well:

Resources for Standard Risk Terms

- ❏ A Guide to the Project Management Body of Knowledge, Project Management Institute

- ❏ PRojects IN Controlled Environments (PRINCE2), Office of Government Commerce

- ❏ 21500:2012 Guidance on Project Management

- ❏ ISO 31000:2009, Risk management – Principles and guidelines,

Be sure to include company-specific and industry-specific acronyms and terms to align with your organizational culture.

Some managers keep a running glossary on easel paper in meetings to capture new terms as they arise and to ensure there's a shared understanding of the terms.

 Keep both a physical and a virtual copy of the risk glossary. It's hard to explain that you're doing effective risk management when your copy vanished with the latest server crash!

 Be careful about using terms from other organizations when they don't align with your organization. Overwriting someone else's common terminology can lead to confusion and conflict.

Risk Attitudes

Every individual, organization, project and environment will have its own diverse risk attitudes. Attitudes are the internal perspective on what risks you choose to worry about and which risks you don't. For example, those in regions of war and conflict may have an attitude that the only risks worth worrying about are those that threaten life and limb. The nature of people's internal attitudes and the external risk sources that may drive them can be maintained in a risk breakdown structure (RBS). The RBS is a hierarchical breakdown of the risks, compartmentalized according to their sources.

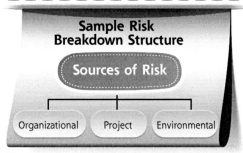

Sample Risk Breakdown Structure

Sources of Risk

Organizational | Project | Environmental

The greater the level of detail in a risk breakdown structure, the more obvious the predetermined sources of risk will be. This allows the people probing the risks on a given project or in a given environment to ask questions beyond "What are the risks?" Instead, the questions become: "What are the risks associated with this process?" "What are the risks of nature?"

Common categories of risk may include:

- Financial
- Legal
- Cost
- Quality
- Environmental
- Management
- Resource/Personnel

The hierarchy of risks can evolve, and this means that as attitudes about risks change over time, new risks can become part of the regular conversation within the organization. For example, the present-day risks of terrorism will change as technology advances. As the environment changes, so will individual and organizational attitudes about risks.

When working on a project, also consider looking at the Work Breakdown Structure (WBS) to identify risk categories specific to the nature of the work.

Creating a Risk Community

Establishing a risk culture, language and environment is built on creating a sense of community. In a small town, everyone knows where the potholes are, where the police set up speed traps, and where the common locations for accidents exist. It's common knowledge. People who do not avoid these day-to-day risks may not be in tune with the community.

 Make sure all of the key people involved have a common understanding of the most frequent and expected risks. It's easy to forget that those new to the risk culture may not know what to expect.

 Too many common risks can also discourage new and different ideas if the common list of risks looks complete.

There are a variety of ways to proactively share information. Some organizations alert others to risk through the use of social media or posters and placards that declare the pitfalls just ahead. These are the equivalent of warning signs along the highway. And while they work, in some cases, team members may stop noticing them after a while so it's important to keep the public warnings fresh and reinforced.

⊗ 🕂 Open every meeting with a "risk minute." A single member of the organization starts the meeting by identifying a common risk associated with the meeting's subject matter and how it should be properly treated. If it's an opportunity, the minute may reinforce/remind others in the organization of the need to look for and exploit opportunities. If it's a threat, the minute may be spent on how to avoid or mitigate it.

Define Risk Roles and Responsibilities

As a critical component of creating a risk community, people's roles and responsibilities need to be defined. This can be as simple as clarifying who will be responsible for which steps in the process moving forward, or as complex as a matrix refining critical risk areas, cross-referenced with those participants who have a clear understanding of the risks in those environments. Risk ownership (ensuring each risk has a principal point of control) is a critical success factor in risk management.

In defining people's risk roles and responsibilities, it's important to consider the entire risk management process.

All of these aspects need to be defined and refined, along with the parties responsible for their successful implementation.

At the same time, it's vital not to overdo risk management. The process should be adapted to the scale of the project and the magnitude of the risks.

Process	Large, Critical or Complex Endeavors	Single-function or Smaller-scale Efforts
Plan Risk Management Chapter 1	The risk management plan is formally adopted and approved at the executive or senior management levels and reflects their specific interests.	The risk management plan is crafted by the manager involved and may or may not be endorsed at a senior management level.
Identify Risk Events Chapter 2	Conducted initially by several stakeholder groups with different stakes in the project. Is repeated on a prescribed schedule and when change is planned or occurs.	Conducted initially by the manager and members of the team. Repeated when major change occurs or is planned.
Identify Risk-Categorization Chapter 2	Done against a risk breakdown structure that reflects the prime sources of risk within the organization.	If needed, sorting risks is based on perceived sources of risk within the effort.

Continued...

Process	Large, Critical or Complex Endeavors	Single-Function or Smaller-Scale Efforts
Analyze and Evaluate Risks — Chapter 3	May involve both qualitative and quantitative tools to determine overall impacts on organizational objectives as well as effort-specific objectives.	Applies qualitative analysis to determine most significant risks.
Plan Risk Responses — Chapter 4	Involves costing individual strategies against the potential return to the organization. Incorporates the inputs of multiple stakeholders representing multiple constituencies.	Involves identifying strategies that will create levels of risk that are acceptable to the organization.
Monitor and Control Risks — Chapter 5	Involves using a risk register to capture the efficacy of the strategies chosen and their deployment. Engages risk owners for ongoing input on success and failure of the strategies selected.	Involves creating tasks for team members to address planned risk responses. Tasks are tracked to completion.
Monitor and Control Risks - Lessons Learned — Chapter 5	Formal debriefs are conducted to determine elements of success that should be repeated in future efforts (and pitfalls that should be avoided).	A post-effort meeting should be held to share insights on accomplishments.

The Risk Management Plan

What is it?

The Risk Management Plan (RMP) lays out the risk processes, tolerances, thresholds and triggers. It documents the organization's, project's or individual manager's sensitivity to risk and creates a risk road map to follow.

Why do it?

The RPM serves both as a general guide on people's attitudes and behaviors, and as a primer on the risk culture for anyone new to the project or organization.

How do I do it?

Risk Management Plan Cycle

Establish Risk Management Objectives

What is it?

Risk management objectives are the targets that the process will ideally achieve. Such targets may relate to opportunities to be realized, risks to be managed or minimized, or tolerances not to be exceeded. The objectives may as simple as "To survive the next six months without being the topic of breaking news." Or the objectives can be as complex as a list of month-to-month cost targets or schedule goals.

Why do it?

The objectives clarify what the organization genuinely cares about when it comes to risk, allowing other aspects of risk analysis to be established, including tolerances, thresholds and triggers.

How do I do it?

1. Define risk management objectives through a series of simple questions:

    o What conditions have to be met for this effort to be deemed a success?

    o What conditions are considered wholly unacceptable in terms of this effort? (Tolerances)

    o Are there any changes in parameters that could alter the answer to either of the previous questions?

All of these questions need to be revisited regularly.

2. Use the answers to these questions as groundwork for developing tolerances, thresholds and triggers that will drive risk management behavior going forward.

Establish Tolerances, Thresholds, and Triggers

Tolerances

What is it?

Tolerances are those points beyond which a project or organization cannot and will not go. These are the absolute limits of what the culture and community can handle or accept.

Why do it?

Individuals and organizations react to risks (favorably or not) and respond according to that reaction. Those reactions represent their risk "behaviors." Tolerances provide the foundation for all discussions on what is and is not appropriate risk behavior in the context of the project or organization. Without them, limits are only discovered when they're actually reached.

How do I do it?

For any of the project objectives, define what is outside the acceptable range in terms of time, cost, or quality. What would cause termination of the project or initiative? At what point would management stop the work?

🏊● Thresholds

What is it?

Thresholds are the safe distance before a tolerance is hit when individuals and organizations should change their behavior because a risk event is either about to happen or is happening.

Why do it?

Thresholds clarify a last-chance effort to alter behavior before a tolerance is reached. They provide an opportunity to stop or alter risky behavior.

🏃 How do I do it?

For each tolerance identified, create a table to establish when behaviors should change (as in the following below). Since people have different attitudes about risk, some individuals will set thresholds closer to the tolerances and some individuals will set them farther from the tolerances. By establishing norms within an organization or project, it's possible to create a degree of consistency in organizational risk behaviors.

Tolerance	Threshold	Trigger
Heart Attack	BP > 190/110	BP > 160/95
Diabetic Seizure	BG > 200	BG > 150
Mini-stroke	C > 240	C> 200

BP= Blood Pressure BG = Blood Glucose C= Cholesterol

Like a doctor's early warnings about health issues, thresholds provide a chance to change behavior before the events actually come to pass.

Triggers

What is it?

Triggers are
the physical
manifestation
of a threshold
being ap-
proached or
breached. At
the side of

many highways, rumble strips provide a warning that
the edge of the road is only inches away, and the car
is about to deviate and slip onto the shoulder.

Why do it?

Triggers are established so everyone has clear warning
that risks are impending. In the highway rumble strip
example, the threshold is probably about a foot away
from the edge of the road. Most drivers, however, won't
know when they're precisely one foot from the shoulder. The trigger (the rumble strip) makes that threshold
evident. Triggers provide unmistakable evidence that
the threshold has been (or is about to be) reached and
that the tolerance (not going off the road completely)
is about to happen.

Triggers may also be used to indicate when there's a
shift in probability or impact.

Identify tolerances first, then thresholds, then triggers.
Test them by asking if the triggers give enough time to
react before the risk becomes reality.

↦ The risk management plan should be readily available to the team. Sharing information about triggers is important if everyone is going to be watching out for them.

↦ Establishing too many triggers or warning signs can create its own set of problems. Some stakeholders become overly nervous and hypervigilant as a result. Other stakeholders become so acclimated to the warnings that they don't notice the triggers anymore.

How do I do it?

Once it's clear what areas cause concern, the key to identifying triggers is to answer the question of "How does the world look different just as the threshold is reached?"

1. Identify tolerances.

2. Define thresholds.

3. Define and choose triggers.

4. Verify that triggers will allow enough time to react before the risk becomes reality.

↦ If there are no clear natural triggers to indicate a risk is happening or may happen, it may become necessary to create them. The roads did not always have rumble strips. But before creating a vast early warning system, ask whether or not the triggers will truly be sufficient to avert a run-in with the tolerance.

Whether those triggers may be qualitative or quantitative is discussed in Chapter 3. Clear numeric scales (like blood pressure) are clear, quantitative values that express differing degrees of the probability of a risk occurring. Qualitative terms can still be clear and objective, but they relate more to experience and conditions rather than absolute values.

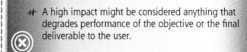

A high impact might be considered anything that degrades performance of the objective or the final deliverable to the user.

Defining Probability and Impact

In most environments, risks are qualitatively assessed as high, medium or low. While such conventions are fine, the risk management plan should incorporate definitions of those terms for both the probability and the impact of a perceived risk.

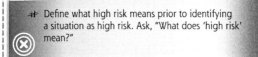

Define what high risk means prior to identifying a situation as high risk. Ask, "What does 'high risk' mean?"

High, Medium and Low Probability

What is it?

It's the likelihood that a risk event and its impact will occur in terms that can be easily evaluated in the course of a discussion.

Why do it?

Weak terms like "very likely" don't provide a lot of value, since they are highly subjective. The more objective the terms, using numbers or criteria, the more effective qualitative analyses will be later.

 How do I do it?

The following samples are representative, and are not intended to reflect a given organization's "right answer."

Example/Sample Terms for Probability

High Probability	Has occurred on more than half of past efforts of a similar nature. Is considered a common and/or systemic risk event.
Medium/Moderate Probability	Has happened more than one time, but happens on less than half of all projects and efforts.
Low Probability	Has happened in this organization once.
Remote Probability	Has never happened in this organization.

The advantage to qualitatively evaluating probability will be discussed in greater depth in Chapter 3. The more that people use the same values (and values that ultimately can be related to numbers) to determine the likelihood of a risk, the more consistent risk assessments will become.

Probability terms can also be related to "standardized" values for later mathematical assessments.

Example/Sample Values for Probability

High Probability	65%
Medium/ Moderate Probability	35%
Low Probability	5%
Remote Probability	0%

The benefit of using consistent definitions for probability is that they can be applied to a broad spectrum of projects that differ in size, volume, cost or effort.

1. Determine if there are consistent definitions of probability in the organization.
2. Establish the definitions to be used on all of the efforts in which you're involved.

High, Medium and Low Impact

What is it?

Just as teams and organizations establish definitions for probability, they also need to establish definitions for what is at stake for a given risk or set of risks.

Why do it?

While the probability of a risk can be consistent from project to project and effort to effort, the impact of a risk can vary widely. A £10,000 potential problem on one project may be considered a cause to stop the endeavor entirely. In another project, this amount might be little more than a rounding error. To be consistent in evaluating risk, the terms for high, medium and low impact are crucial.

*Example/Sample Criteria
for High, Medium, Low Impact of Risk*

High Impact

Cost	= > 10% of remaining contingency budget	By setting the scale against remaining contingency or remaining budget, the scale becomes more sensitive as contingency funds are consumed.
Schedule	Affects the deadline or delivery date	Many schedule problems occur that create headaches without affecting the actual delivery. This is an example of the worst type of schedule delay.
Requirements	Renders the work unusable or worthless	While some risks may limit utility of whatever work is being done, those that make all of the effort for naught are the most catastrophic.
Legal	Prompts legal action	Some organizations have sensitivities to outside influence (like legal) and these should be considered.

Medium Impact

Cost	Everything between high and low impact	The middle level is largely established by first establishing the high level (where thresholds are neared or breached) and the low level of impact (where individuals can generally be trusted to manage their efforts independently).
Schedule		
Requirements		
Other		

Low Impact

Cost	= < 1% of the remaining contingency budget	This should be low enough that even multiple incidents at this level could readily be managed.
Schedule	Does not affect other work	
Requirements	Cosmetic (except when cosmetics are a priority)	
Other	No legal or regulatory effect	

How do I do it?

The relationship between prioritization and tolerances and thresholds are now crucial. If the thresholds have been clearly identified, in many instances they will become the "high" criteria on the High-Medium-Low scale. In many situations, it's not only advisable, but critical to involve customers, sponsors and senior management in establishing the scales. The scales will reflect the overall "risk appetite" of the organization and those responsible for implementation. Consider the following questions:

1. When would you want to be notified without delay of a risk event? **(High Impact)**

2. When would you want any action taken to be managed at a non-management level without your intervention or awareness? **(Low Impact)**

3. What is in between low and high? **(Moderate/Medium Impact)**

The input of those responsible for risk implementation is most important on the impact scales, as it will ultimately determine which risk events may be escalated to a higher management level.

In the previous table, notes are provided to explain the different ways in which the information may ultimately be expressed. These criteria allow for a conversation based on mutual understanding as to which risks have the highest impacts and which are most likely to occur.

The relationship between probability and impact is discussed in greater depth in Chapter 3, as is the relationship to RYG or RAG (red, yellow/amber, green) analysis. RAG analysis is a tool that uses color coding to highlight degrees of risk in a quick, at-a-glance view.

Establish Risk Management Processes
Identifying Participants

What is It?

The Risk Management Plan includes the stakeholders' roles and responsibilities related to risk.

Why do it?

Stakeholders with a wide variety of perspectives have the best information on the nature of the risks and on how to manage them. Some risks will be more readily evident to one group than another. People dealing with accounting and finance have a much better chance of getting early insight on monetary risk than do team members outside those groups. Also, when triggers are identified, it becomes important to pinpoint who will receive the information that a trigger has occurred.

 How do I do it?

1. Find the individual who is best able to identify the early warning signs (the triggers), by working backward from a scenario where the risk event has already occurred. For example, recall the highway driver and the rumble strips. While an attentive police officer might see the car veering off the road if he/she was present, a police officer is not the best candidate to warn the driver. The best candidate to take responsibility for the risk of driving off the road is the driver of the vehicle (even more so than a passenger), since the driver would not only hear the rumble, but would feel the vibration in the seat, the steering wheel and through the brake and gas pedals.

---

2. The questions that need to be answered and incorporated in the RMP in its later iterations include:

○ Who determines that a trigger has occurred?

○ Who needs to know that a trigger has occurred?

○ Who is responsible to take action if a trigger has occurred?

○ Who is responsible for evaluating the trigger's effectiveness in the long term?

The answers to all of these questions may come from the same individual or from different people. This is why this information is crucial in a risk management plan. All of the information that is generated in relation to a risk will ultimately need to be documented and stored. That's the function of the risk register.

The Risk Register

What is it?

The risk register is an electronic document that provides structure for cataloging, tracking and reporting on risk events as more information is gathered about them.

Why do it?

The information you gather will need recording. At this stage in the process, that home is a blank table that reflects the information you want to collect.

How do I do it?

The risk register may be a spreadsheet or any tabular view in project management software or other program. It normally incorporates a variety of elements that afford an at-a-glance perspective on what information is currently available regarding the risks discovered on the project.

Guidelines for the headings of a
Risk Register

Identified Risks
Stated as full sentences, including the causes and effects of those risks

Probability/Liklihood
Often expressed in qualitative terms, e.g., high, medium, low

Impact
Often expressed in qualitative terms, e.g., high, medium, low

Overall Risk or Priority
The ranking (relative or absolute) of the risk in terms of the other risks under consideration

Risk Owner
The individual chartered with implementing any strategies and tracking their outcomes, as well as reporting on the current state of the risk

Strategy/Response
The risk response may be either active or passive, but it should be documented in order to acknowledge that an approach was consciously selected

Review Date
The date on which the risk should be reviewed to determine ongoing probability, impact, and response efficacy

Outcome
The ultimate disposition of the risk event upon completion, including lessons learned regarding strategy implementation

The risk register may be simplified greatly on smaller efforts or efforts where there are time and resources available to address all identified risks.

Finances: Management and Contingency Reserves

One of the key considerations in an RMP is how the organization will deal with the costs of risk, particularly through contingency and management reserves.

What is it?

Reserves are funds that are set aside overtly to ensure that there is money to deal with the inevitable challenges that may arise in the project life-cycle. They come in two forms: management reserves and contingency reserves.

Management reserves are set aside at the top level of an organization to deal with unknown and unknowable problems that surface and may harm a team's objectives.

Contingency reserves are set aside at the project or departmental level to deal with problems that arise in the day-to-day operations of doing business.

Why do it?

Contingency reserves encourage honesty in estimating by virtue of allowing those creating the estimates to realize they will not be forced to live with a budget that assumes a risk-free environment. Managers who consistently have contingency reserves stripped away from their budgets will ultimately attempt to work around the system by embedding hidden reserves in their budgets. With hidden reserves, since they were

Reserves

Management Reserve (MR)

Controlled by management. This is for unknown, unexpected and unpredictable things that come "out of the blue" like a lightning bolt, meteorite, or the bridge that fell when a truck hit the bridge in Seattle on Thursday.

Contingency Reserve (CR)

Controlled by the project, this is for predictable things that may or may not happen like customer changes, team member mistakes, or delayed deliveries.

incorporated in other components of the budget, it's virtually impossible to track consumption. As a result, those hidden contingency reserves are often consumed during the normal life-cycle of the effort without any awareness that they were additional funds intended for use on risks. Management reserves serve a similar function, stopping the practice of putting in extra cash just in case disaster strikes.

In a construction effort, for example, contingency reserves may deal with materials cost overruns or failures.

Management reserves are normally established at the more senior echelons of an organization, and provide coverage for the whole organization. As such, they generally represent a very small percentage of the overall value of the sum of the organization's work and work

Executives

Upper Management

Upper Management

Upper Management

Project Level

Project Level

Project Level

Project Level

Project Level

Project Level

Management Reserve

Contingency Reserve

budgets. This is how management reserves are normally established—a simple percentage of the overall value of the work being done by the organization.

In a construction effort, management reserve(s) might be applied to cover the costs of an act of nature, such as a sinkhole or lightning strike at the construction site.

How do I do it?

1. Contingency reserves can be set up in a variety of ways. The most common way is to use a percentage of project costs, with the percentage based on the relative risk of the project in question (compared to other work being done by the organization).

 Other strategies, such as the use of Monte Carlo analysis or expected value may be applied.

 Some personnel will try to use contingency reserves to fund additional work that wasn't originally in the plan. That's not why it's there. It's important to enforce rules about the proper use of contingency reserves to prevent scope creep.

2. The RMP should include clear direction on how the risk reserves can be tapped, when, and by whom.

3. Any reporting mechanisms related to reserve consumption should also be clearly identified.

● Reassess the Risk Management Plan Cycle

What is It?

The Risk Management Plan should be reevaluated by revisiting the entire Risk Management Plan Cycle in this pocket guide. Determine the frequency and/or circumstances which necessitate the reassessment.

Why do it?

Risk management used too often can lead to a sense of cultural paranoia. Used too infrequently, and crises will evolve without warning or notice.

How do I do it?

1. The frequency of repeating the entire risk process should be based on criteria that may include, (but are not limited to):

○ Complexity
○ Duration
○ Environment
○ Culture

2. Determine if the project or initiative is too close to organizational risk tolerances.

 ➡ If there is a steady progression of risk events moving toward higher levels of probability and impact during a single cycle through the process, or if reserves (management or contingency) are almost exhausted, the organizational tolerances may be about to be breached.

3. Use the following criteria to revisit the RMP when large changes are planned or occur at regular intervals, to be determined.

○ The work has been done successfully in the past.

○ The personnel assigned to the work are familiar with the work.

○ There are processes in place that will allow the work to be consistent with past efforts.

○ There is enough money in the budget and time to recover from potential problems, under normal circumstances.

 If all the criteria above are not met, you should review the Risk Management Plan more often to ensure that the generally higher levels of risk can be managed.

Risk Management Plan Ownership

Once the risk management plan has been written (at least in first draft), some level of peer or management review is appropriate. Getting signatures is a powerful means to affirm that others have both read the document and are willing to accept its guidance on managing risks. While there will inevitably be changes over time, a signature affirms that the approach as laid out to date is viable and mutually acceptable.

Risk Road Map

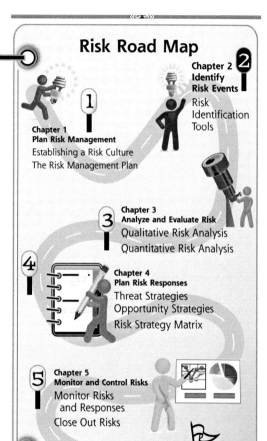

Chapter 1
Plan Risk Management
Establishing a Risk Culture
The Risk Management Plan

1

Chapter 2
Identify Risk Events
Risk Identification Tools

2

Chapter 3
Analyze and Evaluate Risk
Qualitative Risk Analysis
Quantitative Risk Analysis

3

Chapter 4
Plan Risk Responses
Threat Strategies
Opportunity Strategies
Risk Strategy Matrix

4

Chapter 5
Monitor and Control Risks
Monitor Risks and Responses
Close Out Risks

5

TWO

IDENTIFY RISK EVENTS

Risk Identification

Risk is made up of events with varying degrees of likelihood and impact. Good risk identification describes the event that may happen and the impact it may have.

There are many structured techniques to identify risk, including different types of brainstorming. Before you start, be sure you have the "right" people participating. Those "right" people are those with the experience, understanding and knowledge about the risks and the risk environment at hand.

From the simplest to the most complex, the risk identification tools enable a healthy conversation about the world as it could be, rather than the world as it is.

Some of the most common techniques for identifying and sharing risks are:

- Structured Discussion: SWOT Analysis

- Brainstorming Approaches

  - Brainwriting (CTMJ)

  - Brainstorming: Write It, Say It, Slap It™ (PMMJ 2nd edition)

  - Affinity Diagram (MJ2)

- Expert Consensus: Delphi Technique

- Cause and Effect/Fishbone Diagram (MJ2)

These techniques allow you to generate an updated risk register.

#+ In considering the best approach to gather risk data, consider both the skills of the facilitator and the characteristics of the participants. Ask yourselves, "How long will it take? What is the benefit? Is this overkill or will my team be willing to sit through this? Is the risk high enough that I need this much risk assessment?"

 **SWOT Analysis**
(Strengths, Weaknesses, Opportunities and Threats)

What is it?

The SWOT analysis is normally a high-level perspective on the positives and negatives associated with the project or effort you are considering.

Why do it?

SWOT explores the high-level aspects that may influence the overall objectives. It is a powerful early presentation tool, clarifying your rationale for potential risks and risk actions. It can help identify risk categories for brainstorming, but SWOT alone is inadequate for risk analysis.

 How do I do it?

1. Create a four-square grid to highlight the four areas under consideration, Strengths and Weaknesses of the organization on the top half, Opportunities and Threats associated with the project or work on the bottom.

2. Identify individuals who can accurately assess (from a high-level perspective) the information in each of the quadrants.

3. Populate the quadrants with the identified individuals' insights. The more detail, the better.

4. Analyze the SWOT four-square. This is generally done at angles. Strengths are compared with Threats to determine if the strengths may offset some shortcomings that may exist as a result of the effort. Opportunities are examined to see if they create a situation where some of the organization's weaknesses may be overcome. If such an analysis fails to yield any effective comparisons, the question may be asked as to why the effort is being undertaken in the first place. If the work proposed doesn't leverage strengths or offset weaknesses, it may not be logical to pursue.

5. Check the Weaknesses and Threats columns for any common themes. If there are common themes, this should raise "red flags" that serious problems may result in these areas. (The case study of Alpha Corporation has such an example of SWOT Analysis).

Strengths	Weaknesses
•	•
•	•
Opportunities	Threats
•	•
•	•

SWOT ANALYSIS

Strengths

The strengths quadrant is generally focused on the capabilities of the organization, and is not specific to the issue in question. It's an overarching perspective of what the organization does well. The facilitator should ask the questions, "What does the organization do well?" and "Where does it act or respond favorably?"

Weaknesses

The weaknesses quadrant is also focused on the capabilities of the organization and is not specific to the issue in question. It's an overarching perspective of where the organization tends to be challenged. The facilitator should ask the questions, "What does the organization not do well?" and "Where does it act or respond poorly?"

Opportunities

The opportunities quadrant is a laundry list of the positive reasons for moving ahead with the issue or approach in question. The facilitator should ask the questions, "What opportunities will this effort create?" and "What benefits may it bring to the table?"

Threats

The threats quadrant is the list of the negative risks that may influence the objectives of the effort. The facilitator should ask the questions, "What dangers may this effort create?" and "What problems may it bring to the table?"

⊗ The SWOT analysis is a preliminary or early tool in the process of risk identification and is used to highlight the large-scale aspects of the work. It is not effective for detailed analysis.

⊗ For threats and weaknesses that show up in common, upper management should be notified. Common threats and weaknesses may cause the entire effort to fail.

Brainstorming Approaches

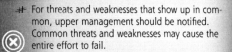

Brainwriting 6-3-5 Method

What is it?

It's a modified brainstorming technique designed to generate a lot of written ideas in a short time frame.

⊗ The name Brainwriting 6-3-5 comes from the process of having 6 people write 3 ideas within 5 minutes.

Why do it?

To provide the time and structure for team members to thoughtfully generate a large number of ideas and to find unusual connections and combinations among those ideas.

Brainwriting creates several powerful benefits:

○ Provides a worksheet for team members to record their ideas.

○ Combines the energy of exchanging ideas and the thoughtfulness of a nonverbal, written process.

○ Defuses emotional issues that may reduce the participation and creative flow of ideas among team members.

○ When compared to classic brainstorming, this tool more consistently builds synergy among team members' ideas

○ As with all non-verbal risk identification techniques, brainwriting limits the sense of blame and/or a self-fulfilling prophecy when sharing risk information.

How do I do it?

1. Assemble the team. The ideal number of team members is six, but a smaller or larger group can also use this tool.

2. Specify the risk question. "What are the risk events and the effect(s) of those risk events that we think could happen?" Each person writes this question at the top of his or her worksheet.

For a different perspective, assign the boundaries of the risk identification—all areas of risk or areas limited to one or more categories such as "legal" or "financial."

3. Complete the worksheets in silence, no discussion. Instruct participants to record both the risk event that may occur in the future and the effect(s) it may cause. Examples:

o Car accident may happen, causing death.

o Car accident may happen, causing damage to the car.

4. Each person writes three ideas in the top row of the worksheet (within a five-minute time frame) then passes the worksheet to the person on the right.

o With each pass, read all the ideas written on the worksheet to stimulate your own thinking, and then generate three more ideas. Remember to:

  o Expand on an idea

  o Write a variation of a previous idea

  o Generate a completely unrelated new risk

6-3-5 Worksheets

Risk Question: "What are the risk events and the effects they may cause?"			
	1	2	3
1	Car accident may happen, causing death.	Car accident may happen, causing damage to the car.	
2			
3			
4			
5			

⊗ ✲ Stuck in developing a risk statement? Ask yourself questions about past projects or other roles in the organization. "If I were management or the customer, what risks would I see? If this was just like my last project, what risks might happen?"

⊗ ✲ As an alternative to writing directly on the worksheet, write each idea on a Post-It™ Note and place it within one of the boxes on a worksheet. The notes can be removed later for sorting and grouping. (See the Affinity Diagram in the MJ2.)

⊗ ✲ Consider using on-line technologies to capture the risk events. Webinar breakout rooms, white boards, and group instant messages can accomplish many of the same goals.

Brainstorming: Write It, Say It, Slap It™ or Type It, Say It, Enter It™, PMMJ 2nd edition

When you need to generate risks in a quick and efficient way, Write It, Say It, Slap It™ or Type It, Say It, and Enter It™ is a versatile and effective tool.

What is it?
It's a process that encourages the free flow of ideas about what risks exist on a project.

Why do it?
The process encourages team members to leverage the ideas of their peers, while also documenting the information.

How do I do it?

1. Specify the risk question. What are the risk events and the effect(s) of those risk events that you think could happen? Instruct participants to record both the risk event that may occur in the future and the effect(s) it may cause.

2. Give each team member a marker and a pad of 3x3 sticky notes or use a virtual whiteboard or text chat, Instant Messaging (IM), etc.

> ⊗ ✢ When using the text chat or IM features, download the transcript before ending the session to document the results.

3. Communicate the boundaries of the risk identification to participants. Are they to brainstorm any risks they can think of, or should they restrict their ideas to risks within a particular category (e.g., internal risks, customer-facing risks, financial risks, etc.)?

4. Start brainstorming to generate ideas.

   a. Team members write their ideas on sticky notes— one idea per note or on the virtual whiteboard.

   b. As each idea is written, someone reads it aloud.

   c. The note just read gets slapped on a piece of easel pad paper or "entered" on the screen.

5. Process the risk events. Discuss, clarify, understand, explain, carefully evaluate duplicates, if any, and group the ideas or decide as appropriate.

When you're brainstorming, keep these guidelines in mind:

o Don't censor or judge ideas.

o All ideas are welcome.

o Don't discuss the ideas during the brainstorming. You will process them later.

o Duplicate ideas are OK. Do not stop if you hear someone say what you are writing. It probably isn't the same risk event.

o Brainstorm as many ideas as possible.

 Brainstorming happens in the right brain. It is not a discussion, not logical, nor linear. Discussion and logical thinking take place in the left brain.

 Beware of the team members who dominate the discussion and exclude others. Afford everyone the opportunity to participate.

Affinity Diagram

What is it?

It's a tool for taking a large number of ideas (like risks) and sorting them into natural categories (MJ2).

Why do it?

It can serve as the foundation for the Risk Breakdown Structure by providing insight into the sources or categories of risk. It can also provide a sense of groups of risks that may have a common solution.

 How do I do it?

1. Use a brainstorming method (Brainwriting 6-3-5 or Write It, Say It, Slap It™) to generate a large number of ideas.

2. Without talking, sort the ideas into naturally related groupings.

> ╫ Rotate posting through the team, not individuals, allowing each team member to post only one or two ideas at a time. This avoids having mostly one team member's ideas indelibly etched on the process.

> ╫ Give team members the latitude to move risks from column to column. If a risk keeps moving, it may be time to create a duplicate sticky note. Place the original in one grouping and the duplicate in another grouping.

What are the risks associated with an outdoor wedding and reception in summer?

It may rain, creating a mad scramble to stay dry

It may be over 100° causing heat stroke

Local wildlife may eat the food, ruining the reception

The ground may be soft, causing problems for the physically impaired

Outdoor facility regulations may not allow for alcohol, forcing a new location

The flowers may attract bees, creating a threat to guests

The bride's dress may drag through the grass, making it look dirty

Insects may attack the guests, causing them discomfort

The event may conflict with vacations, causing a lack of attendance

There may not be power outlets for the lights and music, forcing alternative power sources

The caterer may not serve outdoors, causing the need for a replacement

What are the risks associated with an outdoor wedding and reception in summer?

It may rain, creating a mad scramble to stay dry

The flowers may attract bees, creating a threat to guests

Outdoor facility regulations may not allow for alcohol, forcing a new location

It may be over 100° causing heat stroke

Local wildlife may eat the food, ruining the reception

The caterer may not serve outdoors, causing the need for a replacement

The ground may be soft, causing problems for the physically impaired

Insects may attack the guests, causing them discomfort

The event may conflict with vacations, causing a lack of attendance

There may not be power outlets for the lights and music, forcing alternative power sources

The bride's dress may drag through the grass, making it look dirty

What are the risks associated with an outdoor wedding and reception in summer?

Conditions

It may rain, creating a mad scramble to stay dry

It may be over 100° causing heat stroke

The ground may be soft, causing problems for the physically impaired

Critters

The flowers may attract bees, creating a threat to guests

Local wildlife may eat the food, ruining the reception

Insects may attack the guests, causing them discomfort

Vendors

Outdoor facility regulations may not allow for alcohol, forcing a new location

The caterer may not serve outdoors, causing the need for a replacement

Timing

The event may conflict with vacations, causing a lack of attendance

Facilities

There may not be power outlets for the lights and music, forcing alternative power sources

Image

The bride's dress may drag through the grass, making it look dirty

> It's OK for some risks to stand alone. These "loners" can be as important as others that fit into larger groupings naturally.

3. For each grouping, gain consensus on the type of risks represented within that group, and write a name for the group above it (the header).

Another option is to review the headings and ask if there are additional risks in any/all of the groupings. Are there any other "Image" risks? Are there any other "Timing" risks? And so on.

If your organization does not have a standard Risk Breakdown Structure, capture the header titles in the Risk Management Plan as the key sources of risk identified on the project. Over time, if the same groupings/header titles repeat from project to project, a standard RBS may evolve from the information gathered.

> Consider using an online application-sharing program and the use of PowerPoint or other presentation/graphics software when working virtually. Many "shared whiteboard" applications don't make it easy to move information once it's posted.

Virtual Sessions

1. Generate the risk information in text boxes.
2. Share the application so that others can click on the boxes and move them into groupings that they deem appropriate.
3. Continue to share access privileges until everyone is satisfied with the layout.
4. Save and share the file so that it can be kept with other elements of the risk archive.

Delphi Technique

The Delphi Technique is considered by many to be a risk management "classic."

What is it?
The Delphi Technique is a form of anonymous and remote brainstorming designed to achieve the consensus of experts.

Why do it?
The Delphi Technique allows experts to share ideas and achieve consensus without bruising egos. Brainstorming among experts can be fraught with danger. Some experts have personal or professional biases about their opinions, rendering it difficult to get an objective perspective on other possibilities. Because the experts in a Delphi process never know who the other experts are since it's done anonymously, the biases are removed. The Delphi Technique is also appropriate because of the difficulties in getting experts to participate in group activity due to their differing schedules and work demands.

How do I do it?

1. As with the other brainstorming techniques, identify the key premise of the effort, and provide a format, e.g., "What are the risks associated with XYZ?" Format your answers as **Event** may happen, causing **effect(s)**.

2. Identify experts who are familiar with the nature of the work and/or the environment in which the risks may occur.

3. Draft an e-mail to the experts (anonymously addressed), explaining the process, and requesting their initial inputs on the risks they perceive on the project.

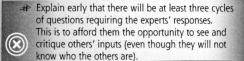

   -#- Explain early that there will be at least three cycles of questions requiring the experts' responses. This is to afford them the opportunity to see and critique others' inputs (even though they will not know who the others are).

   -#- By its nature, the Delphi Technique can become time consuming. With each e-mail, you may need to include a deadline to keep the process going.

4. Review the first set of responses and create an amalgamated list of them. Edit as little as possible.

5. Send a second e-mail to the experts with the amalgamated list, requesting any additions they might identify as well as any concerns or critiques they have for the risk list generated so far.

6. For the second set of responses, repeat steps 4 and 5.

7. Thank the experts for their inputs and incorporate their insights, as appropriate, in the risk register.

Cause and Effect/Fishbone Diagram

What is it?

The Cause and Effect or Fishbone Diagram is a tool designed to highlight the multiple causes (and ideally, the root cause) of a single, crucial effect or outcome. Each "bone" of the Fishbone Diagram highlights different risk areas or sources.

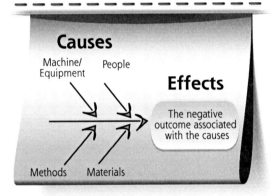

Why do it?

The Fishbone Diagram is used to identify, explore and graphically display, in increasing detail, all of the possible causes related to a problem or condition to discover the root cause(s).

1. Enables a team to focus on the content of the problem, not on the history of the problem or the differing personal interest of the team members.

2. Creates a snapshot of the collective knowledge and consensus of a team around a problem. This builds support for the resulting solutions.

3. Focuses the team on causes, not symptoms.

Root cause is difficult to know in a project because you usually do not have multiple data points. In operations, this data is more often available. See the MJ2 for instructions on how to construct the Cause and Effect Diagram.

The risk identification tools in this chapter can all be used to generate a large number of ideas of risk events. The more categories of risk that are applied, and the more perspectives that are considered, the more risks will be generated. In organizations previously unfamiliar with the process, the problem is not whether or not a risk list can be generated, but instead what to do with the sheer volume of risk events produced.

Updating the Risk Register

What is It?
The risk register was originally established during risk management planning. The updated version is a version populated with the information generated during risk identification.

Why do it?
The register is evolutionary, growing over time as you generate more information. It provides a home for risk information.

How do I do it?
Most simply, the risk register is now more than just a spreadsheet of information. It now actu-

ally contains the well-defined, clearly-stated risks that were generated during risk identification. Some risk registers will separate cause and effect, while others simply include a list of risk events.

1. Populate the "Risks" column of the risk register spreadsheet with clear risk statements.

2. Populate the "Groupings/Categories" column of the risk register spreadsheet with categories associated with the individual risks.

While those are the two most significant pieces of information now available to populate the risk register, other information may have come out of these early steps. Some of the other information that may already be generated includes:

1. Identifying the risk owners (if there are any clear owners as yet identified) as the individuals responsible for shepherding the risk through the remainder of its life. As soon as the risk is identified, you may know the owner.

 A temporary risk owner can be identified if a permanent risk owner has not yet been chosen. Certain risk events have clear owners that are readily tied to them, while others can not be assigned until risk responses have been selected.

2. Establishing triggers may also be defined at this point if the root causes were identified during a Fishbone Diagram analysis. As part of the risk identification brainstorming processes, some participants may identify early warning signs that a risk is happening or imminent.

Risk Road Map

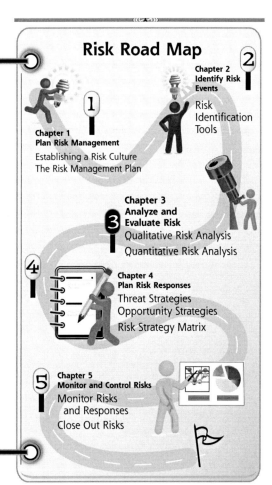

Chapter 1
Plan Risk Management
Establishing a Risk Culture
The Risk Management Plan

Chapter 2
Identify Risk Events
Risk Identification Tools

Chapter 3
Analyze and Evaluate Risk
Qualitative Risk Analysis
Quantitative Risk Analysis

Chapter 4
Plan Risk Responses
Threat Strategies
Opportunity Strategies
Risk Strategy Matrix

Chapter 5
Monitor and Control Risks
Monitor Risks and Responses
Close Out Risks

THREE

ANALYZE AND EVALUATE RISK

Whole-project risk versus individual risks

Making the decision between qualitative and quantitative

Qualitative Risk Analysis: The process of prioritizing risks for further analysis or action by assessing and combining their probability of occurrence and the impact of each risk.

Quantitative Risk Analysis: The process of numerically analyzing the effect of identified risks on overall project objectives.

  Conducting whole-project analysis versus individual-risk analysis

There are situations where comparative analyses of risks on a project-wide scale are required, rather than looking at independent risks within a project. While many of the concepts discussed thus far apply, it's important to define which type of analysis you are doing. For some organizations, whole-project evaluations may be conducted before the project is officially chartered.

What is It?
It's the determination that the evaluation (quantitative or qualitative) is going to take into account either the whole effort or just one risk driven by that effort.

Why do it?
It's difficult to manage all risks to any effort, so you'll need to identify which are the most significant or important. If you know why you're using a particular tool, it becomes much easier to decide what data and what skills you need to keep risk in check.

How do I do it?

1. Ask what the results will be at the outcome.

2. If the information will be used to assess the impact of individual events on the objectives of the effort, look at it from an individual risk-evaluation perspective. Otherwise, consider whole-project evaluations.

3. Once that's determined, establish what data is available. If there is a core of clear statistical history available, consider the quantitative. Otherwise (and more commonly), you use the qualitative evaluations.

Qualitative and Quantitative Tools: How and When to Apply Them

Probability and Impact Matrix

The matrix can be displayed as shown below or can be split out between opportunities and threats.

	Qualitative	Quantitative
Single-Risk Evaluation	Probability and Impact (PxI) Matrix	Expected Value
		Failure Mode and Effects Analysis (FMEA)
		Monte Carlo
Whole-Project Evaluation	Balanced Scorecard	Monte Carlo
		Expected Value

What is it?

The Probability and Impact Matrix is a color-coded graphic used to plot individual risks into Red, Yellow or Green zones, with red reflecting those risks that need the most or most immediate attention.

It's important to recognize that the qualitative probability scale would be somewhat evenly stepped (e.g., 30%, 60%, 90%), while the impact axis would be stepped by orders of magnitude (e.g., 2, 4, 8) if mathematical comparisons were to be applied.

○ Probability would be
   Low = 15%
   Medium = 50%
   High = 80%

○ Impact would be
   Low = 2
   Medium = 4
   High = 8

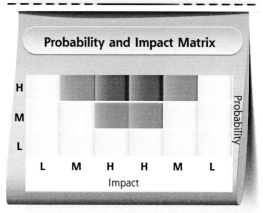

Probability and Impact Matrix

Probability

H
M
L

L   M   H   H   M   L

Impact

Why do it?

The Probability and Impact Matrix provides a clear, simple interpretation of which risks are "significant" and which risks do not merit immediate time and attention.

How do I do it?

The values for High, Medium and Low (and remote, as applicable) for probability and impact were established in the risk management planning stage. Using those criteria, you can populate the grid with individual risks, placing them in their zones as appropriate.

If the original identification was done on yellow sticky notes, for example, those notes can be placed on an easel pad in the appropriate part of the grid.

Probability and Impact Matrix

		Threat		
Prob-ability	**H** 80%			Red
	M 50%			Yellow
	L 15%			Green
		L 2	**M** 4	**H** 8
		Impact		

* The words Red, Yellow, and Green are shown to depict the colors that the boxes should be colored.

Plotting Probability and Impact

Probability %	Impact 2	Impact 4	Impact 8
80	High Probability Low Impact	High Probability Medium Impact	High Probability High Impact
50	Medium Probability, Low Impact	Medium Probability Medium Impact	Medium Probability, High Impact
15	Low Probability, Low Impact	Low Probability Medium Impact	Low Probability, High Impact

Impact

The probability values vary from organization to organization.

⚡● Balanced Scorecard

What is it?

Enables a leadership team to evaluate the status of implementation and make whatever adjustments are necessary to achieve desired long-term goals with regard to risk.

Why do it?

○ Provides an update to management on the key indicators of strategic success.

○ Informs management of the success or failure of strategic initiatives and the cause-and-effect connections.

○ Serves as a decision-making device for senior leadership.

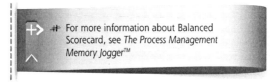

+> # For more information about Balanced Scorecard, see *The Process Management Memory Jogger™*

Expected Value (EV) or Expected Monetary Value (EMV)

What is it?

Expected value or expected monetary value is a risk-analysis tool that multiplies the probability of a risk's occurrence times the impact of the risk to achieve a quantitative value for how much the risk is worth. In other words, if the probability is accurate and the risk was taken thousands of times, the expected value reflects the average cost of an instance of taking the risk. Some organizations use EMV to determine aggregate contingency reserve.

Why do it?

No risk is going to hit every time. But you still need ways to figure out how much time or money (on average) needs to be set aside to intelligently accommodate the risk. You can't afford to set aside the full value of each risk you may run into, but to intelligently assess what's a fair value for risk mitigation (like a preventive action), transfer (like insurance) or contingency, you need to know the average value for the risk itself.

Probability X Impact = Expected Monetary Value (EMV)

Example:
Risk of rework after testing. Probability = 35%. Cost of rework = $24,000. EMV = (0.35) x $24,000 = $8,400

How do I do it?

The hardest part of calculating expected value is determining a data source for the values. In most organizations, hard statistical data on impact is limited and data on probability is even harder to come by. Gathering impact data is normally a function of determining how much repair, remediation or failure would ultimately cost if a threat becomes reality.

Probability data is tougher to develop. Ideally, it would come from hard statistical data, which is rarely available in a unique business environment. Some organizations blend the qualitative and quantitative analyses by setting down consistent values to be used for all probabilities assigned under the risk-management plan.

Probability (from the RMP)	Quantitative value (to be used when statistics are unavailable)
High	65%
Moderate	35%
Low	5%
Remote	0%

These examples reflect how an organization can use qualitative values to apply in a quantitative situation.

FMEA (Failure Mode and Effects Analysis)

What is it?
Acknowledges both risk events and their multiple potential impacts to the project or organization.

Why do it?
It allows you to look at risk events from multiple dimensions, including their multiple impacts, as well as other aspects, including detectability. With the deeper data set, it provides a better understanding of the risks themselves.

Item of Process Step	Potential Failure Mode	Potential Effect(s) of Failure	Severity	Potential Cause(s)	Occurrence	Current Controls	Detection	RPN	Recommended Action	Responsibility and Target Date	"After" Action Taken	Severity	Occurrence	Detection	RPN

Project _____ Team _____ Date _____ (original) _____ (revised) _____

Total Risk Priority Number =

"After" Risk Priority Number =

How do I do it?

1. List the tasks, project work packages or risk areas in the first column of the chart.

2. For each item in the first column, identify a potential risk event (failure mode) or events that could have a negative impact on the objective if the risk event occurs.

3. For each item in the second column, identify the effects of the failure, recognizing there may be more than one effect for each risk event. Then rate their severity.

4. Identify the causes of these effects and rate their probability. (Column is labeled "occurrence.")

5. In the Detection column, rate your ability to detect each item in column 2.

6. Multiply the three numbers (for severity, occurrence, and detection) together to determine the risk of each failure mode. This is represented in the chart as a risk priority number (RPN).

○ Use the rating scales for severity, occurrence, and detection shown on the next few pages.

⊹ Develop your own scales for severity, occurrence and detection or use the following sample scales. Be sure they are aligned with the metrics established within the Risk Management Plan (RMP).

⊹ Do not change the scales once they're set. Like resetting the sights on a rifle each time you miss the bull's-eye, the scales can lose their value if they're recalibrated.

Severity = Likely impact of the failure?

	Rating	**Criteria:** A failure could:
Bad	10	Cause the end of the project or organization. Cause death.
	9	Force major restructuring of the project or organization. Cause injury.
	8	Cause lawsuits.
	7	Cause loss of customer.
	6	Cause failed functionality.
	5	Cause customer complaints.
	4	Cause performance loss.
	3	Cause internal rework.
	2	Cause internal concerns.
Good	1	Cause no visible impact.

7. Identify ways to mitigate or eliminate risks associated with high risk priority numbers (RPNs).

8. Re-score those failure modes after you put your risk strategies in place.

9. The remaining columns in the table are completed when risk responses are applied to evaluate the efficacy of the responses.

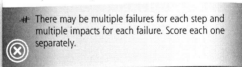

There may be multiple failures for each step and multiple impacts for each failure. Score each one separately.

Occurrence = How often have similar failures occurred in the past?

	Rating	Time Period	Probability
Bad	10	Last quarter	Happens more than 1/2 the time.
	9	Last year	Happens more than 1/2 the time.
	8	Last 5 years	Happens more than 1/2 the time.
	7	Last quarter	Happened more than once, but not more than 1/2 the time.
	6	Last year	Happened more than once, but not more than 1/2 the time.
	5	Last 5 years	Happened more than once, but not more than 1/2 the time.
	4	Last quarter	Happened more than once, but not more than 1/2 the time.
	3	Last year	Happened once.
	2	Last 5 years	Happened once.
Good	1	Last 5 years	Never happened.

Detection = How likely are you to know if the potential failure has occurred or is imminent?

	Rating	Detection
Bad	10	Will be completely invisible until after it has transpired.
	9	Will become visible as it is happening.
	8	Will become sufficiently visible to identify, but no action can be taken before occurrence.
	7	Will be visible in time for last-minute action with limited efficacy.
	6	Will be visible in time for last-minute action with high efficacy.
	5	Will be visible in time to implement planned mitigation and response strategies.
	4	Will be visible in time to allow limited discussion to consider mitigation & response strategies.
	3	Will be visible in time to allow limited discussion to consider mitigation & response strategies.
	2	Will be visible in time to allow for complete proactive avoidance.
Good	1	Will be clearly identifiable with more than enough time to proactively act in any manner desired.

Monte Carlo Analysis

What is it?

A computer-driven analysis of multiple versions of possible realities. It takes into account hundreds or thousands of different simulations to determine the likelihood of reaching a given result.

Why do it?

It takes into account the range of possibilities for individual events, evaluating their influence on the entirety of cost or schedule outcomes. It allows you to answer the question: What are the odds you'll be able to hit this cost or schedule target?

How do I do it?

The key is having a program do a proper analysis, having the right inputs, and then *you* gather duration ranges, cost ranges, dependencies, and likely distributions of outcomes for work on the project. A computer simulator then evaluates those different possibilities and determines how likely an overall cost or schedule target is.

1. Determine Durations and Cost Ranges

A duration or cost range is the range of realistic possible outcomes for a project or effort. It's gathered by asking those responsible for the work for the best and worst cases (as well as the most likely) for an element of work. This information is normally gathered in a simple, tabular format.

Best Case	Most Likely	Worst Case
$$ or Time	$$ or Time	$$ or Time

2. Establish Distributions

If team members are unaware of distributions or statistics, that's OK. Getting the three data points for a triangular distribution (in the previous table) is often sufficient. If team members know the distribution, it provides more accurate information. The most common distributions accounted for in the tools include:

a. Normal Distribution

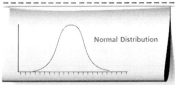

The normal distribution accounts for those situations where team members normally know what the outcomes will be, but there are sometimes situations where there are outlying incidents—just as likely good as bad. It's a classic bell curve.

b. Beta Distribution

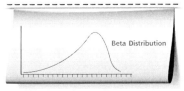

Beta distributions are used in situations where the outcomes tend toward either the positive or the negative end of the spectrum, but there is still a remote chance they could wind up at the other end.

c. Uniform Distribution

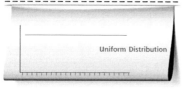

Uniform Distribution

Uniform distributions are especially appropriate when there's very little history to work with. If a worker only knows how well and how poorly a piece of work may evolve, a uniform distribution may be appropriate. Only the best and worst cases need be accounted for here. The distributions assume any outcome on the spectrum is just as likely as any other.

3. Create/Affirm Dependencies

Part of a thorough Monte Carlo analysis will be the relationships among the tasks. If you identify what comes first and what comes next, Monte Carlo analyzers can take those relationships into account in establishing the range of possible outcomes.

What do the tools do?

Monte Carlo simulators take the information provided and create a version of how the work might turn out. Then they create another. And another. They do it a thousand times over, with each possible outcome as a separate "hit" in the analysis. Eventually, a probability density function is created. That's a curve that shows how likely given outcomes might be.

In this example, the thin line in the middle reflects the original duration of the project as projected in project

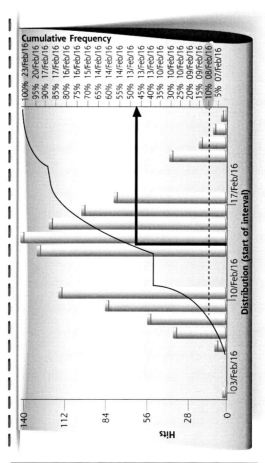

management software. The Monte Carlo analysis indicates that there's about a 46% chance that the work will be completed within that time frame.

The curved line that slopes up from left to right shows the relative likelihood that different durations will be achieved. Add four days to the original duration in the middle? The probability of achieving the duration is up to over 90% (as the sloped line indicates).

How do I use this information?

With a schedule or cost curve, management and customers can now find out the relative likelihood of meeting deadlines or meeting cost targets. The same analysis can also provide you with task-specific information about which tasks are most frequently driving cost or schedule increases. That's achieved through another aspect of a Monte Carlo analysis, called a Tornado Diagram.

 **Tornado Diagram**

What is it?

A Tornado Diagram is an output from a Monte Carlo Analysis that indicates how often a given task is responsible for driving up costs or increasing the overall project schedule.

Why do it?

By knowing which tasks are the most common "offenders" on the schedule or budget, it's easier to assign the right staff to them. For tasks that consistently drive costs and schedules, more skilled and seasoned personnel may be appropriate to minimize risk. For tasks that rarely impact cost and schedule, there's an opportunity to assign less skilled team members.

How do I do it?

The interpretation may seem painfully obvious. In the following example, Task 5 is driving longer schedules 62% of the time. Task 3 is driving them only 1% of the time. You probably want to assign the most skilled resources to Task 5 and the less skilled staff to Task 3.

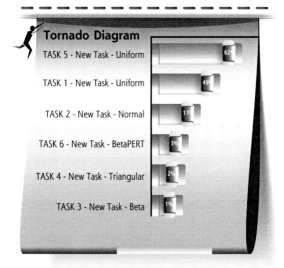

Tornado Diagram

TASK 5 - New Task - Uniform — 62%

TASK 1 - New Task - Uniform — 49%

TASK 2 - New Task - Normal — 17%

TASK 6 - New Task - BetaPERT — 3%

TASK 4 - New Task - Triangular — 2%

TASK 3 - New Task - Beta — 1%

Interactive Risks

Many of these math models become either invaluable or moot as risks potentially interact with other risks. In many situations, a single threat will not sink a project. Instead, it may be that many different risks must come together for an effort to fail. While the Monte Carlo analysis actually addresses many of the quantitative concerns associated with interactive risks, you still need to ask how to deal with multiple risks occurring at the same time. Sometimes you need to ask the questions on probability, impact, expected monetary value, and organizational tolerance from the perspective of more than one risk. When you do that, a different perspective on the acceptability of threats sometimes will surface.

Picking the Right Tools

TOOLS	Qualitative	Quantitative
Single-risk Evaluation	Probability and Impact (PxI) Matrix	Expected Value
		Failure Mode Effect Analysis (FMEA)
		Monte Carlo
Whole-project Evaluation	Balanced Scorecard	Monte Carlo
		Expected Value

While this is sound guidance on choosing the tools to apply in each situation, consider the availability and quality of data. In many organizations, true statistical data doesn't exist. In those instances, it's best to fall back to the qualitative tools, and use the quantitative only if/when you have the data.

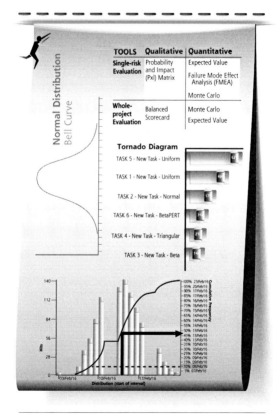

TOOLS	Qualitative	Quantitative
Single-risk Evaluation	Probability and Impact (PxI) Matrix	Expected Value
		Failure Mode Effect Analysis (FMEA)
		Monte Carlo
Whole-project Evaluation	Balanced Scorecard	Monte Carlo
		Expected Value

Tornado Diagram

TASK 5 - New Task - Uniform

TASK 1 - New Task - Uniform

TASK 2 - New Task - Normal

TASK 6 - New Task - BetaPERT

TASK 4 - New Task - Triangular

TASK 3 - New Task - Beta

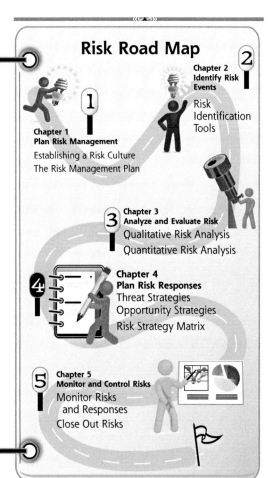

Risk Road Map

Chapter 1
Plan Risk Management
Establishing a Risk Culture
The Risk Management Plan

Chapter 2
Identify Risk Events
Risk Identification Tools

Chapter 3
Analyze and Evaluate Risk
Qualitative Risk Analysis
Quantitative Risk Analysis

Chapter 4
Plan Risk Responses
Threat Strategies
Opportunity Strategies
Risk Strategy Matrix

Chapter 5
Monitor and Control Risks
Monitor Risks and Responses
Close Out Risks

FOUR

PLAN RISK RESPONSES
Selecting Risk Strategies

What is it?

Because risk is a future phenomenon, strategies are the proactive steps that you can take to deal with the impact of threats or opportunities.

Threat Strategies

- Avoidance
- Acceptance (passive and active)
- Mitigation
  - Minimizing Probability
  - Minimizing Impact
- Risk Transfer

Opportunity Strategies

- Acceptance
- Enhancement
    - Enhancing Probability
    - Enhancing Impact
- Sharing
- Exploitation

The beauty of the multiple strategies is that they ultimately represent options for you in your decision-making.

Threat Strategies

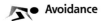 **Avoidance**

What is it?

Avoidance is the act of ensuring that no matter what happens, there is no way that the risk can hurt you. Either the probability or impact is reduced to zero.

Why do it?

Avoidance is appropriate whenever the risks involved are too great. A classic example followed the Bhopal disaster, where thousands died from a leak of methyl isocyanate. Since then, most responsible pesticide manufacturers avoid this risk by not using the chemical in any of their manufacturing processes. The probability of death is reduced to zero.

 **Acceptance**

What is it?

Acceptance is the act of inaction. While acknowledging that a threat may affect the objective, you take no action. That inaction can be, oddly enough, passive or active. Passive acceptance is to take no action and only document that the threat exists. With active acceptance, you take no action proactively, but document a game plan to deal with the threat if or when it comes to pass.

Why do it?

Acceptance is the single most common strategy for threats. It is used when you believe the threat can be managed after it comes to pass. It is also used when the risk is external and unpredictable. A meteor strike is a classic example. There's nothing you can do about it proactively, and its effects are so global that there's no sense in creating a separate strategy just for that risk.

Risk Register

Event	Overall Risk	Strategy
Team member may fall, causing injury	Low	Acceptance - Dial emergency services if required

How do I do it?

Accepting risks begins when you document their existence in the risk register. If you accept risks with no contingent responses, then the documentation renders them as passively accepted. If, however, (as in the example above), you identify some reactive response should the risk occur, you document the contingent response and actively accept the risks.

> ❌ For actively accepted risks, communicate the contingent responses widely in the organization. Team members can't react appropriately if they do not know the response!

Mitigation: Minimizing Probability

What is it?

It is the act of ensuring there is a lower likelihood that a threat event will occur.

Why do it?

If the threat is within tolerances, organizations may choose to live with the potential impact, as long as it is less likely to occur. Mitigating probability is used in situations where risks are extremely likely and the probability can be reduced dramatically, and in situations where a modest reduction in probability makes them more politically palatable.

> Don't let team members or management be misled into believing that a reduced probability is the same as an avoided risk. Some stakeholders can misconstrue the nature of reduced probability.

How do I do it?

Probability can be modified when you evaluate the environment and determine the conditions that cause probability to increase. By changing those conditions, you reduce the likelihood.

Mitigation: Minimizing Impact

What is it?

The act of ensuring that if the threat comes to pass, the amount at stake is not as severe as it would have been without the action.

Why do it?

In some instances, threats that exceed organizational tolerances can be minimized to a degree where they are considered acceptable. In such situations, minimizing the impact may be the only motion forward.

How do I do it?

As with probability, the first step is to look at the environment to determine what aspects of the threat hurt most. In car accidents, for example, the greatest threat to most drivers is to go through the windshield. Once the major influence is identified, mitigation is a function of minimizing the impact of that influence. Seat belts achieve that goal. While they do not reduce the probability of an accident, they do reduce the impact.

Probability or Impact? For many mitigation strategies, it's not a matter of probability or impact. It's both. The key is not to confuse these strategies with risk avoidance, as the threat may still come to pass and could still influence your outcomes.

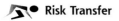 **Risk Transfer**

What is it?

Transfer is the act of shifting the ownership and re-sponsibility for a threat to another party, for financial reasons or outsourcing the risky part to a third party with expertise and more capability. It is noteworthy that risk transfer often mitigates risks (minimizing probability and/or impact). While the strategies can technically fall into two categories, you want to ex-plore as many strategies as are reasonable.

Why do it?

If the burden of a threat is too heavy to bear, rather than dropping a project, an organization may choose to share the potential impact of the threat with a third party.

 How do I do it?

Insurance, warranties and guarantees are the classic examples of transfer, although some organizations try to achieve transfer by shifting risk back on their customers or on subcontractors.

- Transfer is rarely complete. While insurance may alleviate a financial burden, you may still face some of the political ramifications of a risk.
- Mitigation and transfer tend to be the most expensive of the threat strategies.

Opportunity Strategies

 Acceptance

What is it?

An acceptance strategy for an opportunity is an acknowledgment that the opportunity exists and there is a possibility that you will be able to take advantage of it.

Why do it?

Acceptance is the single most common strategy for threat or opportunity. As a simple acknowledgment, no additional action is required, and thus no additional expense is incurred.

How do I do it?

The only action required to determine whether or not you're using an acceptance strategy for an opportunity is to ask if you're in the running to take advantage of it. For example, you cannot accept the opportunity of winning the lottery without purchasing a ticket. Once your status as a participant is documented in the risk register, no further action is required.

 **Enhancing Probability**

What is it?

Enhancing the probability is increasing the likelihood that an opportunity will come to pass.

Why do it?

In some instances, the cost of making something more likely to happen is well worth the investment.

Some organizations will submit multiple proposals in response to a request for proposal (some as the prime contractor and others as subcontractors) because they see the opportunity as too lucrative to pass up. There's still no guarantee their proposal will win, but they want to improve the odds.

How do I do it?

In most instances, enhancing opportunity is accomplished through redundancy. More entries into a drawing, more approaches for a problem, more versions of a text—all are examples of how the probability of success can be enhanced.

Enhancing Impact

What is it?

Enhancing impact is much more challenging than enhancing probability. This is where a favorable outcome becomes even more favorable by virtue of a proactive approach.

Why do it?

If the probability of success is deemed sufficiently high, you may want to leverage the opportunity to get more of the positive outcome. It should be noted, however, that the outcome is still not a "sure thing."

How do I do it?

Enhancing impact is more daunting than enhancing probability. Rather than changing the odds, you find ways to ensure that if the opportunity happens, it will work even more greatly in your favor.

This often means a larger investment in the outcome in the form of purchasing a larger stake. State lotteries in the United States often achieve this by selling lotto tickets with "doublers," which cost more, but double the payout of certain prizes.

Sharing

What is it?

Sharing is the act of partnering with some other person or organization to increase the probability of achieving the desired outcome. It's the classic "two heads are better than one" argument.

Why do it?

In situations where opportunities are attractive, but you don't have the ability to make them more likely, sharing creates a situation where you can leverage the opportunities of others in your favor.

 How do I do it?

Sharing is a process that follows four simple steps:

1. Identify a potential partner who has a better chance of realizing the opportunity than you do.
2. Identify who will be responsible for which aspects of the opportunity.
3. Identify how any positive outcomes will be shared (50/50? 60/40?), and how credit will be assigned.
4. Document the nature of the arrangement.

A certain degree of trust is essential to any sharing arrangement.

Exploitation

What is it?

Exploitation is when there are still a variety of different ways an opportunity could hit, but every possible outcome is covered (and will always lead to a gain or opportunity). In horse racing,

Opportunities

Proposal Alpha & us

Proposal Gamma & us

Proposal Beta & us

1

2

3

it would be placing a bet on every horse, but with one key difference. No matter which horse won, you'd have to get back more money than you invested. A more business-oriented example is to partner with all three bidders on a contract so that no matter who wins the bid, you're in on the opportunity.

Why do it?

Exploitation is a strategy that requires only an up-front investment to win. In its truest sense, it's a no-lose approach. If the situation presents itself, exploitation is a sure thing.

How do I do it?

This is the hard part of exploitation strategies. They don't present themselves too often. Because of their nature, most opportunities present the chance that there's a way to lose (or not gain). The heart and soul of doing exploitation is identifying situations where all of the possible outcomes are positive. That's pretty rare.

Risk Strategy Matrix (or Pugh Matrix)

Once a variety of strategies have been identified, the next challenge is trying to discern which strategies are the best. The Pugh Matrix is a tool that enables the decision to discern the strategies.

What is it?

The matrix is a grid that displays the major risks on one axis (as well as the impacts on time and cost), and the strategies that could be applied on the other axis.

Why do it?

The matrix provides a clear indication of which strategies apply most broadly across a variety of different risks. It minimizes the situations where individual risk strategies are developed for each and every risk. It clearly identifies the strategies that have the greatest impact.

How do I do it?

1. Build the graph and include space for cost and time considerations with the risk events.

2. Identify the top risks that you hope to address through consistent strategies (often the high-high risks identified during analysis).

3. Populate the grid with the risks.

4. Ask: For each strategy that will avoid, accept, mitigate or transfer the first risk, will the strategy have a positive effect or a negative effect? Put plus-

ses below the risks that are positively influenced by
the strategy and minuses below the risks that are
negatively influenced by the strategy. This is best
done by a team, as there will be different perspectives on the relative influence of the strategies. The
plusses or minuses can also be accompanied by
values (+1, +3, -4, etc.) based on the relative impact
of the strategies.

> If a strategy will have a positive influence at first,
> but will have a negative influence in the longer
> term, consider using +/– in the appropriate box
> in the grid. Similarly, if a strategy will have a
> negative influence at first, but will have a positive
> influence in the longer term, consider using
> –/+ to indicate that situation.

5. Continue to populate the grid with strategies.
   Evaluate strategies based on the number of plusses
   and the strategy's acceptability within the organizational culture.

Risk Strategy Matrix (Pugh Matrix)

Response Strategies	Team members may get stuck, causing delays	The customer may feel unappreciated, causing termination of the contract	Demand may increase, causing an inability to meet demand	Facilities may not be adequate to meet demand, causing delays	New processes may make some staff obsolete	Cost	Time
More staff	+		+		+	–	–/+
Hire a consultant	+	+	+			–	–
Have regular customer meetings		+				–	–
Build a second facility			+	+		–	+
Fire poor performers	–					+	

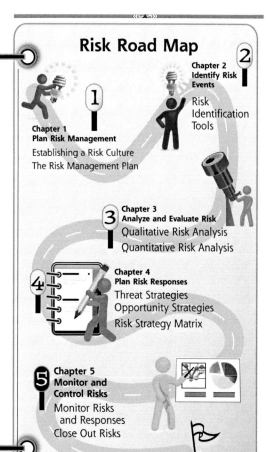

Risk Road Map

Chapter 1
Plan Risk Management

Establishing a Risk Culture
The Risk Management Plan

Chapter 2
Identify Risk Events

Risk Identification Tools

Chapter 3
Analyze and Evaluate Risk

Qualitative Risk Analysis
Quantitative Risk Analysis

Chapter 4
Plan Risk Responses

Threat Strategies
Opportunity Strategies
Risk Strategy Matrix

Chapter 5
Monitor and Control Risks

Monitor Risks and Responses
Close Out Risks

FIVE

MONITOR AND CONTROL RISKS

As the Deming quality cycle suggests, you should Plan, Do, Check, and Act (PDCA). As with that cycle, the thrust behind risk control is repetitive action. That repetition ensures you have the processes in place and revisit them repeatedly. For all aspects of risk control, you need to identify the individuals or areas of the organization who will be responsible to revisit each step in the process. Therefore the information is still timely, being addressed and communicated at an appropriate level.

Who does it?
At a global level, the project manager or the manager of the effort is responsible. Some organizations have risk departments and risk executives, most of the basic risk components are actually addressed by people with direct oversight of the work. In fact, if the "work" is a single work package or task, the person responsible for these risk reviews may be the individual worker, rather than senior-level management.

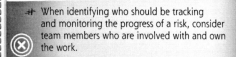

+ When identifying who should be tracking and monitoring the progress of a risk, consider team members who are involved with and own the work.

The person at the lowest reasonable level should complete these reviews since he or she likely has the highest visibility on what's going on and how the risk climate has evolved since work began.

When to do it?

At the very least, a mid-point review is appropriate, or when the environment changes significantly. On work spanning more than three months, additional reviews are probably apt, unless the project is unusually low-risk. For multi-year projects, a once-a-quarter visit to the risk content and process is a reasonable minimum. A positive aspect of a risk review on a well-understood and well-managed effort is that the reviews give you an opportunity to give all involved in managing the risks accolades for their performance.

The reviews may also give you a chance to escalate (or re-escalate) older risks that may have been overlooked by senior management. Do not wait until a crisis to perform a risk review, you have the chance to raise concerns without the concurrent sound of alarm bells.

Controlling the Risks

Perhaps one of the hardest things to remember in risk management is that risks eventually expire and do not remain risks forever. When they occur, they become issues. Risks are future events. Issues are realized. Risk control is about the maintenance of risk documentation and capturing the environment and history when risks convert to issues.

Managing the Risk Register

What is it?

The risk register should now be populated with a wealth of information. Probability, impact, overall risk, strategies,

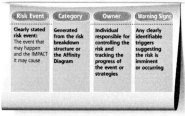

Risk Event	Category	Owner	Warning Signs
Clearly stated risk event: The event that may happen and the IMPACT it may cause	Generated from the risk breakdown structure or the Affinity Diagram	Individual responsible for controlling the risk and tracking the progress of the event or strategies	Any clearly identifiable triggers suggesting the risk is imminent or occurring

and risk owners should have already been identified for each risk.

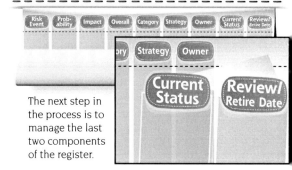

Risk Event	Prob-ability	Impact	Overall	Category	Strategy	Owner	Current Status	Review/ Retire Date

The next step in the process is to manage the last two components of the register.

Why update the register?

Track risk status and set up review dates. When you have a fresh status, you can see that risks and the probability of occurrence evolve over time, becoming more or less probable and impacting. By keeping track of the current status of the risks, you can prepare fellow workers to deal with the challenges or allow them to breathe easy (if the threats are lower than expected).

How do I do it?

1. Determine whether or not the original status of the risk has changed. An environmental review may show that the nature of the risk, its probability and impact have all remained static. If the status has changed, then document the date and the nature of the change.

Status Note

Date: May 29, 2014

Probability adjusted from "High" to "Remote"

Risk owner notified

The change in status should include any actions you have taken or will take to modify the roles and responsibilities associated with the risk event.

---

2. Exclude this step if the risk owner is doing your status update. Notify the risk owner of any change in status. Note that the risk owner is notified before making the final modifications to probability and impact. As the owner has a unique perspective on the risk, he or she may disagree with changes or provide additional insight that should be recorded.

3. Modify the probability, impact and overall risk accordingly, recalibrating the list to identify a new "top list" of risks, based on the adjustments.

4. Review the strategy to determine if the planned strategy is still applicable. If a risk has become more of a threat, you may need a more aggressive response. Similarly, if a threat has lessened, then your earlier aggressive stance may not be needed.

 Don't forget that some risks actually go away entirely. In such cases, the status should be updated to "Retired," coupled with the retirement date. In associated notes and lessons learned, any rationale for the retirement might be helpful in determining how to retire such risks more quickly in the future.

5. Determine the next occasion for a timely review of the risk's status.

6. Continue the process until all of the timely risks have been reviewed.

7. Check the list "Review/Retire Date" column to record the retire or next review date.

⚲● Risk Audits

What is it?

Formal assessments of the risk process and the risk management plan (RMP) which are designed to ensure that the process and plan reflect the risk culture and the relative levels of risk associated with the project or the organization as a whole.

Why do it?

By conducting an audit of the risk process, you determine if the process is doing what it is supposed to do. By validating the process, you determine what works and what doesn't, to improve long-term ability to manage risks.

⚲ How do I do it?

There are two types of risk audits. The first is an audit of the process as it is applied to a particular project. The second is an audit of the risk management plan's efficacy in representing the organizational risk culture.

Conducting a Process Audit

1. Review the key tools and techniques of the process. This step is generally made up of a documentation, timing and process review. It should answer the questions:
   o What tools are we using to identify risks?
   o When and how are we using those tools?

- Do we have the risk register?
- Is it populated with all of the appropriate data?

2. Document the answers to the questions.

3. Determine if the answers to those questions reflect the process you planned to use (in the RMP).

4. If yes, then continue to step 5. If no, document the variations from the process and makes plans on how to change the way you follow the process to be compliant in the future.

5. Review the risks and the strategies implemented. Answer the questions:

- Was the body of risks identified relatively comprehensive? (Were there no gaping holes?)

- Did the risk(s) never happen?

- Did the risk owners follow through on the assigned strategies? (Did they act as prescribed, when prescribed)?

- Were all the significant risks that happened identified by the process?

- Did the strategies achieve the anticipated results?

6. For any "no" answers, the risk process needs to be reviewed to determine how to achieve a "yes" answer the next time the process is conducted.

If all of the answers are "yes" answers, then the successes of the process should be documented, and any exceptional successes should be captured in Lessons Learned.

When you decide who will do the audit, consider how sensitive the risks are. You may need internal auditors due to security concerns, but external auditors (where they're available and appropriate) can bring another perspective to the situation that otherwise could easily be missed. External auditors don't have to be external to the organization. They may be those who understand risk, but are not directly involved with the project.

Auditing the Risk Management Plan

How do I do it?

The primary difference between a process audit and an audit of the risk management plan is that the risk management plan's perspective arises from organizational attitudes about risk.

1. Determine the aspects of the risk management plan that will be reviewed. These primarily include the definition of terms and the established tolerances, thresholds and triggers.

2. Gather project documentation, and compare references to risk and risk actions to the aspects identified in step one. If the definitions in the project documentation reflect the definitions in the risk management plan, and if the tolerances, thresholds and triggers drove the appropriate responses, no further action is required.

3. (As required.) If the definitions, thresholds, tolerances and triggers in the RMP do not match the actions on the risks, document corrective action to bring those actions into alignment with the RMP in the future.

Every term, phrase and/or item that will be audited should be highlighted in the RMP. The use of bold, color, or italics can serve as a reminder that the item/phrase is or has been reviewed in the audit.

Items and terminology included in the audit of the RMP are risk, issue, risk register, high probability, low probability, high impact, low impact, acceptance, mitigation, transfer, and avoidance. The definition and application of the terms should be validated during the audit process.

 ## Risk Register Updates

What is it?

At regular review cycles and when significant change is imminent, you will update the risk register. Updates are an opportunity to reflect on the information in each column of the risk register to ensure that the data (and its relative influence on the project) hasn't changed.

Why do it?

Not all of the components of the risk register update are necessarily required. Some organizations use simplified versions of the risk register, and in those cases, the additional elements of the register included here would not be germane.

Risk conditions can change quickly. Probability of occurrence and/or the impact can increase or decrease. The risk register update ensures focus on the risks that are of the greatest potential importance, be it by virtue of probability and/or impact.

Risk Event	Category	Owner	Warning Signs
Clearly stated risk event: The EVENT that may happen and the EFFECT it may cause	Generated from the risk breakdown structure or the Affinity Diagram	Individual responsible for controlling the risk and tracking the progress of the event or strategies	Any clearly identifiable triggers suggesting the risk is imminent or occurring

How do I do it?

A review of the risk register is a systematic review of each of the data points in each of the columns on the risk register. It is the single most important step in risk control.

Reviewing the Risk Name/Event

Risk Event	Category	Owner	Wa...
Clearly stated risk event: The EVENT that may happen and the EFFECT it may cause	Generated from the risk breakdown structure or the Affinity diagram	Individual responsible for controlling the risk and tracking the progress of the event or strategies	Any ider trig: sug: the imr or o

- It is critical to state the risk events clearly enough to allow thorough analysis as the work progresses.

- It's easy to use brief statements early in the project, but as work evolves, the definitions should become more readily and thoroughly understood.

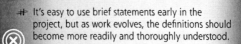

- You may need to clarify some of the risk events during risk control. Understanding the nature of the concern associated with the risk event and its effect(s) is imperative. If the nature of the risk hasn't changed, and the description is clear, no change is required.

If the nature of the description has changed, or can be made more clear, you should update the risk register accordingly. The risk owner must approve changes since he or she will be responsible for the effort associated with the risk as now described.

Risk Event

Clearly stated risk event: The IMPACT may happen and the EFFECT it may cause

Category

Generated from the risk breakdown structure or the Affinity Diagram

Owner

Individual responsible for controlling the risk and tracking the progress of the event or strategies

Warning Signs

Any clearly identifiable triggers suggesting the risk is imminent or occurring

Cultural and organizational risks can result in a radical change in the perceived categories of risk. Prior to 2001, very few organizational risk category listings included terrorism. Now it's a virtual standard. The key in updating risk categories is to ensure that there has been a dramatic enough shift to warrant a change in the established categories or that enough risks have migrated into a new category to warrant creating one.

In addition to the information that goes in the risk register, any time the risk category is adjusted, risk ownership should be revisited.

 Risk ownership is tied to either ownership of the deliverable or the risk environment. In most cases, risk ownership will be guided by who owns the deliverable. In other cases, however, the risk owner will be the person who manages the culture or environment in which the risk can develop.

Some categories of risk have specific owners, and if the current risk owner is not well-versed in the new category in question, it may be time to shift to another risk owner. The categories may shift when significant cultural events occur or when the same groups of topics show up time and time again.

 This is an opportunity for praise, as well as pragmatism. It's a chance to let risk owners know that you are watching their efforts, and (assuming they've been doing their jobs) to heap praise upon them.

Reviewing the Risk Owner

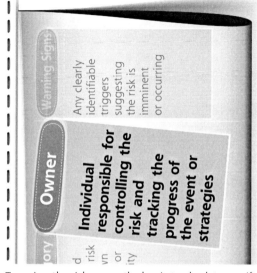

To review the risk owner, the key is to check to see if he or she is still aware of the responsibilities as the risk owner.

Has the risk owner been:

- Updating risk status?
- Monitoring any triggers and thresholds?
- Ensuring implementation of strategies, as appropriate?
- Communicating changes to the appropriate channels?

If all of the answers are "yes," then you likely don't need to shift risk ownership. However, if the risk owner has been unable to pursue those roles, it may be time for a change. If the risk category has shifted to take it out of the owner's realm of expertise, it may be time to move to another owner. As risk owners shift, notify other team members about the change in roles and responsibilities.

Reviewing the Warning Signs or Triggers

If warning signs were not readily identified early in the project, this review becomes an opportunity to update or improve. During the life of a project, new perspectives can arise that shift the nature of the warning signs. Low or high-level concerns raised by vendors or customers may prove to be critical indicators of trouble. Conversely, some early concerns may wane, causing the team to realize that certain participants' input was not crucial.

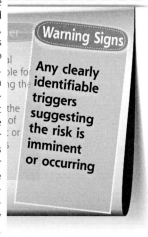

Warning Signs

Any clearly identifiable triggers suggesting the risk is imminent or occurring

As warning signs and triggers are adjusted and documented, immediately notify those affected.

Reviewing the Probability

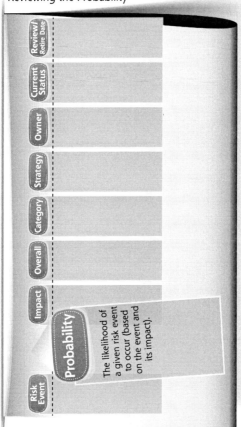

Risk Event	Probability	Impact	Overall	Category	Strategy	Owner	Current Status	Review/Retire Date
	The likelihood of a given risk event to occur (based on the event and its impact).							

The likelihood/probability of any risk event may change over time. The probability of risks can increase or decrease when the window in which the risk can occur becomes shorter. It can also change as the environment around the risk event changes. In order to review probability, you should ask a few key questions:

- Has the environment changed?

  - Customers?

  - Team members?

  - Management?

  - Physical location?

  - Culture?

- Has the risk event occurred (either here, or in other organizational efforts)?

- Has the nature of the risk event changed?

On the last question, that ties back to any changes in the description of the risk event or its impact. If either of those descriptions have changed, it's possible that there's also a change in the probability. Ultimately, any changes here will spur change in the "Overall Risk" category.

Reviewing the Impact

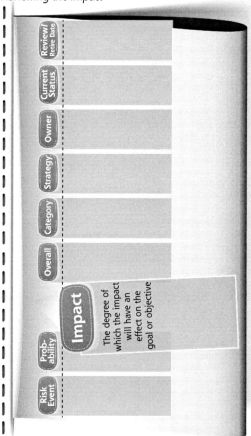

Risk Event | Prob- ability | Impact — The degree of which the impact will have an effect on the goal or objective | Overall | Category | Strategy | Owner | Current Status | Review/ Retire Date

Early in any effort, a change in requirements generally has a nominal impact. Changes can often be incorporated without extraordinary effort. By contrast, in the last days of a project, a change in requirements can have a very large impact.

Because of this, the impact review is the most important of any review of the risk register. It is the component most likely to change over time and it's the most noticeable.

Any changes to the impact column should reflect the definitions created in the original (and now updated) risk management plan. The changes should incorporate the latest thinking about what represents a high risk to the objectives, and the latest descriptions of the risk event (if that description has changed since the beginning of the project).

Once updated, the impact column should reflect the current perspective on how greatly (or how little) a given event will impact the objective.

Reviewing the Overall Risk

As overall risk is a function of risk events, probability and impact, the overall risk score will be adjusted using whatever process you establish to determine risk priorities, for example, weighted or ranked.

Reviewing the Overall Risk

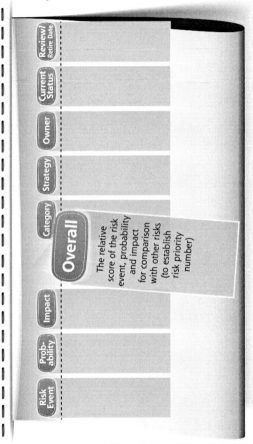

Risk Event	Prob-ability	Impact	Overall	Category	Strategy	Owner	Current Status	Review/ Retire Date

Overall

The relative score of the risk event, probability and impact for comparison with other risks (to establish risk priority number)

Reviewing Overall Risk

Process Examples	Approach	Rationale	Outcome
Expected Value/ Expected Monetary Value	Probability times impact (Qualitative or Quantitative)	Generated an "average" value of the risks considered (if the effort was repeated multiple times)	A lower value than the full value of the risk, but a value that takes both probability and impact into account
Cumulative	Probability PLUS impact (Used only with Qualitative value of H, M, L scaled to numeric values)	Provides a relative value of the risks when comparing them with the other risks in the project to determine which risks should be dealt with first	A qualitative value that generally rates probability more importantly than expected value for organizations that are highly risk-averse
Averaged	Probability PLUS impact divided by 2 (Used only with Qualitative value of H, M, L scaled to numeric values)	Provides a relative value of the risks when comparing them with the other risks in the project to determine which risks should be dealt with first. The only difference is that it provides a context for the high-medium-low scale consistent with that scale for probability and/or impact	A qualitative value that generally rates probability more importantly than expected value for organizations that are highly risk-averse

Process Examples	Approach	Rationale	Outcome
Weighted	Probability times (*X* times impact)	By weighting the impact as either greater than or less than 1, an organization can modify its risk values. An organization that believes impacts are critical and cannot be ignored might set the value as high as 2, putting a dramatic emphasis on impact. An organization that believes that impacts are often overrated might set the value at 7 or 8, creating a lower relative scale	If this effort begins with qualitative values (real monetary values for impact and/or time), then the outputs can be used to establish contingency budgets. If the effort begins with qualitative values, then the sum of the outputs can be used to generate a relative risk priority for this project vis a vis other projects in play or under consideration

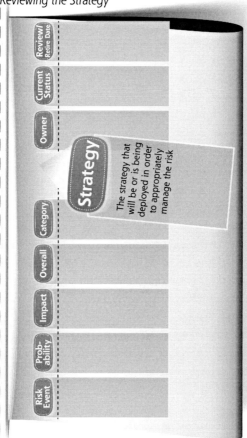

Review/Retire Date

Current Status

Owner

Strategy

The strategy that will be or is being deployed in order to appropriately manage the risk

Category

Overall

Impact

Probability

Risk Event

The strategy review is largely dependent on the nature of the original strategy you chose. It can be as simple as *"Do we want to change this?"* to a comprehensive assessment of the cost, effort and time associated with implementation and the benefits thereof. Beyond that, however, it's important to consider the implications of reviewing each of the different strategies. Each involves asking a slightly different set of questions. For all of the questions, a "yes" answer indicates that the current strategy is probably sufficient and will not require change.

Opportunity Strategies

Acceptance

- Is the opportunity something that would still benefit the organization?

- Are we still in a position to receive those benefits?

- Are we still oriented to simply allow the opportunity to occur if it occurs?

- Are we still satisfied with the opportunity if it occurs?

Enhancement

- Are the efforts we're undertaking still increasing the probability and/or impact?

- Is the opportunity still worth that investment of time, money and/or effort?

Sharing

- Does the partnering arrangement put us in a more likely position to benefit from the opportunity than if we were alone?

- Is the opportunity worth that investment of time, money and/or effort?
- Does the partner make us look good? Increase our credibility? Do no harm?

Exploitation

- Does the approach still cover all possible outcomes, with each having a potential benefit to the organization?
- Is this approach cost-effective and time-effective, while covering every possible outcome?

Threat Strategies

Acceptance

- Is the threat still within our tolerance levels?
- Is accepting the threat more cost-effective and time-effective than any alternatives?
- If the threat occurs, will the project, the organization, and the team that withstands the impact still be successful?

Avoidance

- Is the threat severe enough to alter our approach/ or kill the project altogether?

Mitigation

- Do our existing strategies still minimize the probability and/or impact of the threat?

○ When minimized, is the threat within our tolerance levels?

○ Is the approach creating new, unintended consequences that are worse than the original risk?

○ Can we still afford the time/cost/effort of the mitigation?

Transference

○ Has the party to whom we transferred the threat taken steps to keep us within our risk tolerances?

○ Are they fully aware of their responsibilities?

○ Is the supporting documentation in place sufficient to ensure legal liabilities have been transferred?

For some specific risks, there may be additional questions. However, the key is to ensure that existing strategies (particularly the most overlooked— acceptance) are sufficient to protect the organization and the project from undue harm and to ensure the optimization of any opportunities.

Review of Current Status

Status reports are, by their nature, snapshots of a moment in time. They simply reflect the condition of the risk since the last status review. Options may include (but aren't limited to):

Unchanged – The nature of the event, its probability and impact have seen no modification since the last time around.

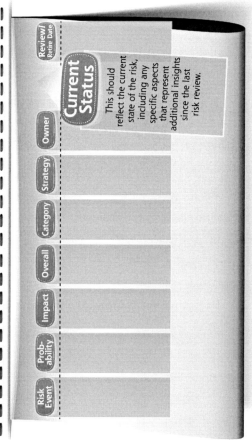

Risk Event	Prob- ability	Impact	Overall	Category	Strategy	Owner	Review/ Retire Date

Current Status

This should reflect the current state of the risk, including any specific aspects that represent additional insights since the last risk review.

Changed – The nature of the event, its probability and/or impact have been modified since the last review. This should include notes regarding the nature of the change. Newly "critical" or "high-priority" risks should be escalated immediately to the manager or project manager's attention.

Managed – The risk strategies applied have had the desired effect, and the risk no longer poses a significant threat to the project.

Retired – The risk has been retired.

Work with the risk owner to develop the status update. For risks that have fallen into the "managed" category, you can be less vigilant.

 Risk Retirement

What is it?

Risks may reach a state where they no longer have influence over a project. Risk retirement happens when you remove a risk event from the risk list entirely and exclude it from future risk reviews. You can retire risks for a single project or from the organization as a whole, depending upon which is appropriate. For example, if a company was consistently reviewing the risk of a particular class of lawsuits, it might retire the risk if the courts declared that any such lawsuits were inherently illegal.

Why do it?

As each risk must have an owner, there is some inherent time and effort consumed by each identified risk. Removing a risk from the register means that resources are free to take on other commitments.

Answer this simple series of questions about the risks under review:

1. Does the risk event still exist, given the nature of the environment, the culture and the project?

2. Is the probability greater than zero? By definition, a probability of zero is not a risk as a risk event is uncertain.

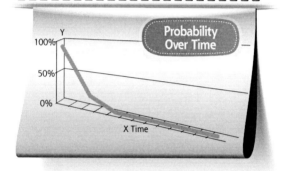

3. If the risk happens, is the impact worth worrying about?

A "no" answer to any of those questions indicates that the risk is ready for retirement.

You should note the retirement date and any lessons learned regarding the risk. If specific actions led to the retirement, you should catalog them, since they represent critical learnings, which may be exploited.

Lessons Learned

What is it?

Lessons learned about risks include the mechanisms, strategies, approaches, techniques and tricks that make themselves evident (as helpful or hurtful) during the evolution of a risk event.

Why do it?

Lessons learned provide valuable insight on how others can use or avoid the learnings. They create organizational history/memory. They are invaluable intellectual property that differentiate the capabilities of one organization from the next.

How do I do it?

The simplest of the strategies is to encourage all project participants and stakeholders to post or report a lesson learned as soon as it is identified. When you or your peers discover it, they should document:

1. The context and environment that makes the risk event that drove the lessons learned more likely.

2. The way in which the lesson learned affects the risk event.

3. How others can effectively apply the lesson learned.

4. Any special conditions or circumstances that make the lesson learned more effective.

5. Contact information of the person who submitted the lesson learned, in case more information is required.

6. Any searchable keywords that should be used in data storage so you and others can find the lesson learned.

The benefit of well-documented lessons learned is sharing organizational memory and building knowledge management, which is something that most organizations only do when they have had a significant failure. Have you ever heard of an organization launching an investigation of what happened when something was wildly successful, exceeding expectations? Well-captured lessons learned create a distinctive and long-lasting competitive advantage to organizations willing to invest the time in ensuring they happen.

Ideally, the lessons learned add not only internal value, but value to the profession, as well, becoming best practices that others may adopt.

Risk Reassessment

As cited earlier, risk is a cyclical process. You repeat all of these steps as needed. One of the keys is to ensure that, per the risk management plan, you repeat the steps with sufficient frequency that they adequately cover or manage the risks. While the schedule for risk reassessment is a component of the risk management plan, implementation falls under risk control. The key is simply to ensure that it actually takes place when change is planned, when change occurs, and at regular intervals.

Risks are not static. The conditions for impact and probability and the environment can change quickly and often, and those who remain in touch with risks as situations evolve are those who can command and lead, rather than be reactive. Awareness is key to stay in step with the risks, the risk environment, and the culture. And when you are risk-aware, you have the opportunity to appear genuinely clairvoyant in your ability to keep work, projects and organizations free from catastrophe. You have the special opportunity to become the owner of your own future.

Risk Management Plan Cycle

Conclusions

"Conclusions" is the least perfect word for these closing paragraphs, as risk is genuinely never concluded. There is no end to risk. And that's why managing it is crucial to your long-term success. With no management process, there is little hope that you can rein in risk to a consistent level. No one can hope to conclude risk. People can, however, hope to keep it sufficiently in check that managers, organizations, teams and families can cope with the remaining pressures of the day-to-day risks present in the world. That's the true goal here—risk management.

As the authors of this work, we hope that you will take advantage of our willingness to provide support to you as our end users. If we can afford you any additional insight or assistance in implementing these practices, we are just an e-mail away at carl@carlpritchard.com. As you implement these practices, we remain optimistic that your risks will be better and more consistently managed.

CASE STUDY

The Alpha Corporation

Organization Mission & Vision with Risk Considerations

Our Mission: To build components as fast as they can be built, while adding shareholder value and creating a global brand.

Risk Culture: If a risk slows down the process, it's a threat. If it enhances shareholder value, it's an opportunity. If a risk hinders the organization's ability to brand the company around the world, it's a threat. These are the major concerns of executive management.

Project Objective: To create a larger organization through a merger with the Beta Corporation, integrating Beta's lean, quick-response practices with Alpha's existing processes and practices. The effort will also leverage the economies of scale of uniting the administrative functions of the two organizations. The project is to be completed within one year at a cost of under $1,000,000.

Project Risk Culture: If budget overruns exceed $1,000,000, the project will be deemed a failure. If the merger is not complete within a year, the project will be deemed a failure. If the merger does not create a single, seamless organization with one set of administrative functions, the project will be deemed a failure.

Risk Terms

Acceptance: The practice of acknowledging a risk's existence, but taking no action proactively. See also Active Acceptance.

Active Acceptance: Acknowledging a risk's existence and creating a strategy that will be implemented only if and/or when the risk event becomes a reality (issue).

Arcana: Risks that are identified but by virtue of their extraordinarily remote probability or their insignificant impact, they are traditionally acknowledged, accepted and marked for review only during comprehensive risk audits.

Audit: A practice of reviewing to determine if all risks have been documented properly and catalogued with the intended responses. Any post-response actions are also documented, including efficacy of the strategies and the ultimate outcomes.

Risk Breakdown Structure

- - - - - - - - - - - - - -

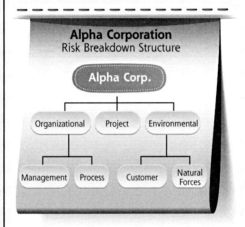

Alpha Corporation
Risk Breakdown Structure

Risk Management Objectives

Current Effort: Merge with the Beta Corporation.

Success Criteria and Constraints: Alpha Corporation must remain a viable entity. The integrated company must have higher earning potential than the existing Alpha Corporation. The integration must be complete in one year.

Tolerances: These are conditions that are completely non-tolerable to the organization. There cannot be any negative press about the organization's financial integrity. There cannot be any physical injury to anyone in either organization as a result of the merger. Any single risk event costing more than $1,000,000 or causing the one-year target date for the merger to be missed.

Risk Management Plan

Current Effort: Merge with the Beta Corporation.

Tolerances: One-year deadline. No more than $1,000,000 for a single risk event. Not one physical injury. Profitability.

Thresholds: A delay on any critical path activity (driving the end date), any risk identified with an apparent impact of $500,000 or more, a near-miss event, an alteration to the overall market or market structure.

Triggers: Warning alerts from project management software, financial risk assessment for a single event (or overall from a Monte Carlo analysis) of $500,000 or more, any exclamation of surprise that physical injury was avoided, articles in the business media relating to Alpha or Beta's market space.

Terms (IMPACT)

High: A risk event creates a situation where time, cost and/or delivery objectives cannot be met.

Medium: A risk event creates a situation where time, cost and/or delivery objectives may be impeded, but they can eventually be met.

Low: A risk event creates a situation where time, cost and/or delivery objectives may be affected, but will not directly influence the outcome of any of the three on project completion.

Terms (PROBABILITY)

High: More often than not.

Medium: Anything between high and low.

Low: Seen it happen once in similar projects here or elsewhere.

Rare/Remote: Never seen it happen.

Risk Review Cycle

Project: Merge with the Beta Corporation.

Review Plan: The project is expected to span one year, but represents work of a nature never taken on before by the Alpha Corporation. The risk management process shall be reviewed as follows:

- Risk Register: Monthly reviews

- Risk Management Plan: At the completion of months 1, 3, 6, 9 and 12.

Risk Terminology

High	Has occurred on more than half of past efforts of a similar nature. Is considered a common and/or systemic risk event.
Medium	Has happened more than once.
Low	Has happened once on projects of a similar nature.
Remote	Has never happened here.

Impact

High	Cost	= > $15,000.
	Schedule	Affects the deadline or delivery date.
	Requirements	Causes the merger not to happen.
	Other	Prompts legal action.
Medium	Cost	Between $501 and $14,999.
	Schedule	May/may not affect the deadline or delivery date (as yet unclear).
	Requirements	May influence the merger outcome but will not stop it.
	Other	May prompt a legal review.
Low	Cost	= < $500
	Schedule	Does not affect other work.
	Requirements	Merger will continue without changing legal terms or conditions.
	Other	No legal or regulatory effect.

Contingency Funds and Access

Contingency funds have been set aside in the amount of $100,000 to deal with unforeseen circumstances within the project scope. The merger manager shall have access to said funds through the Finance Department, charging all funds drawn against contingency to Charge Code C-AB-MGR-315-MO-USE. Single-event charges to said fund in excess of $15,000 shall be authorized by the merger manager with signed approval of C-level staff only.

Risk Cycle

The risk process will be revisited as follows:

1) Any time there is a change involving $25,000 or more, moving the deadline, or a shift of more than two staff resources occurs or is planned.

2) The risk register content will be reviewed and updated at least every other month.

3) The risk management plan and its contents will be reviewed semi-annually.

Approvals

This plan was approved by: Manny Zhur, CEO; Ian Stine, Division Chief; and Sam Dwich, Beta Liaison.

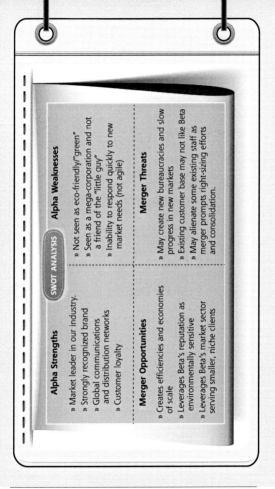

SWOT ANALYSIS

Alpha Strengths

» Market leader in our industry.
» Strongly recognized brand
» Global communications and distribution networks
» Customer loyalty

Alpha Weaknesses

» Not seen as eco-friendly/"green"
» Seen as a mega-corporation and not a friend of the "little guy"
» Inability to respond quickly to new market needs (not agile)

Merger Opportunities

» Creates efficiencies and economies of scale
» Leverages Beta's reputation as environmentally sensitive
» Leverages Beta's market sector serving smaller, niche clients

Merger Threats

» May create new bureaucracies and slow progress in new markets
» Existing customer base may not like Beta
» May alienate some existing staff as merger prompts right-sizing efforts and consolidation.

6-3-5 Case Example

The Tale:

Alpha Corporation is planning to create a larger organization through a merger with the Beta Corporation, integrating Beta's lean, quick-response practices with Alpha's existing processes and practices. The effort will also leverage the economies of scale of uniting the administrative functions of the two organizations and is to be completed within one year at a cost of under $1,000,000.

The Time:

The team met for an hour following an "Our New Beta Friends" briefing.

The Task:

1. Assemble the team and clarify the concern

The organization has to have the project complete within one year, and any merger is fraught with risk. The team's mission is to generate a clear list of risk events (coupled with their impacts) so that they can be included in the risk register and dealt with appropriately.

2. Complete the 6-3-5 worksheets.

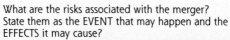

What are the risks associated with the merger?
State them as the EVENT that may happen and the
EFFECTS it may cause?

	1	2	3
1	Government regulators may intervene, causing delays	Team members may get sick, forcing a re-staff	Management may drop the project entirely, causing a loss of morale
2	Beta may change the terms of the agreement, causing legal problems	Alpha's and Beta's information systems may not talk to each other, creating a new expense	The board may determine the merger is not in the best interests of Alpha, causing the project to be dropped
3	Accounting may discover irregularities in Beta's books, causing delays and possible project cancellation	Alpha may change the terms of the agreement, causing legal problems	Beta team members may not cooperate in sharing information, causing delays
4	Additional requirements may develop late in the project, causing rework and delays	Beta's accountants may discover irregularities in the books, causing delays and project cancellation	Data from Beta's systems may go corrupt when ported over to Alpha's systems

Continued...

What are the risks associated with the merger?
State them as the EVENT that may happen and the
EFFECTS it may cause.

	1	2	3
5	The merger may not achieve the cost savings anticipated, reducing the value to both sides	The vast sea of paperwork required by regulators may prove overwhelming, causing deadlines to be missed	Alpha team members may not cooperate in sharing information, causing delays
6	The two sides may not be able to concur on a new name, creating a conflict in corporate branding	Data from Alpha's systems may be corrupted by the importation of Beta data	The new brand may force a change in stationery, causing tons of paper and business cards to be wasted

*3. Analyze the ideas and select the obvious
"high-highs."*

The Tally:

The team's brainwriting effort pointed out the high
level of influence of the government regulators on
the process, and a little post-meeting research

yielded insight that those regulators had asserted themselves on more than half of their most recent merger reviews. Also, both sides in the merger have an extensive history of modifying requirements mid-stream, leading to extensive rework. These issues were determined to be the most crucial low-hanging fruit from the exercise.

Alpha-Beta Merger

In this example, note how all of the smaller "bones" in the fish relate to those they branch from. They are causes of causes. Also note that there is a repeating theme of "Budgets." Because it appears on more than one branch, it may be more than just a cause. It may be a root cause of some of the problems.

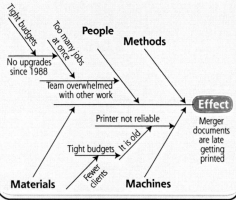

Preliminary Risk Register (post-Identification)

Risk Event	Category	Owner	Warning Signs
Printer may break down, causing late document delivery	Machines	Rufus, Print Shop	Poor production values on preliminary printed materials
Regulatory demands may increase, delaying team efforts	Methods	Machines	News articles on heightened regulation
Beta team may not cooperate in information-sharing, causing delays in implementation	People	TBD	TBD

Alpha Merger - Affinity Diagram

External/Government	Legal	Technical
Government regulators may intervene, causing delays	Beta may change the terms of the agreement, causing legal problems	Alpha's and Beta's information systems may not talk to each other, creating a new expense
	Accounting may discover irregularities in Beta's books, causing delays and possible project cancellation	Data from Beta's systems may go corrupt when ported over to Alpha's systems
	Alpha may change the terms of the agreement, causing legal problems	Data from Alpha's systems may be corrupted by the importation of Beta data.
	Beta's accountants may discover irregularities in the books, causing delays and project cancellation	Printer may break down, causing late document delivery

Continued...

Alpha Merger - Affinity Diagram *Continued*

Management/ Management Objectives	Resource	Requirements
Management may drop the project entirely, causing a loss of morale	Team members may get sick, forcing a re-staff	Additional requirements may develop late in the project, causing rework and delays
The board may determine the merger is not in the best interests of Alpha, causing the project to be dropped	Beta team members may not cooperate in information -sharing, causing delays	The vast sea of paperwork required by regulators may prove overwhelming, causing deadlines to be missed
The merger may not achieve the cost savings anticipated, reducing the value to both sides	Alpha team members may not cooperate in sharing information, causing delays	The new brand may force a change in stationery, causing tons of paper and business cards to be wasted
The two sides may not be able to concur on a new name, creating a conflict in corporate branding.		

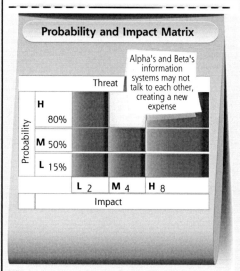

Alpha Merger

Probability and Impact Matrix

Alpha's and Beta's information systems may not talk to each other, creating a new expense

Risk Strategy Matrix (Pugh Matrix)

Response Strategies	Printer may break, causing late document delivery	Regulatory demands may increase, delaying our efforts	Beta team may not cooperate in information-sharing, causing delays in implementation	Alpha's and Beta's information systems may not talk to each other, creating a new expense	Alpha may change the terms of the agreement, causing legal problems	Time	Cost
Minimize probability – Buy back-up for equipment	+	O	O	+	O	–	–
Minimize impact - Hire a support lawyer just for the merger	O	+	+	O	+	-/+	–
Transfer – Hire liaisons for both sides	O	+	+	O	O	–	–
Minimize probability – Create new company, eliminate existing companies	+	O	+	+	+	–	–
Minimize probability/impact – Freeze company activities until merger complete	O	+	+	+	+	–	–

©2013 GOAL/QPC

Risk Monitoring and Control

Risk Event	Probability	Impact	Overall	Category	Strategy	Owner	Current Status	Review/ Retire Date
Regulatory/ demands may increase, delaying our efforts	H	H	H-H	External	Accept: Assign Marty to watch & report	Marty	No change to date	Retire Jan 1st (date of conversion to new company)
Beta team may not cooperate in information-sharing, causing delays in implementation	M	H	M-H	Beta	Mitigate - Sofia assigned as a liaison	Sofia	Sofia hosting bi-weekly meetings	Review Jan 1st
Alpha's and Beta's information systems may not talk to each other, creating a new expense	M	H	M-H	Technical	Mitigate - Sofia assigned as a liaison	Sofia	Agenda item at bi-weekly meetings	Review End of QTR (September 30)

Updated Risk Register

Category	Strategy	Owner	Current Status	Review/Retired Date
			Late additional requirements have not occurred. Reduced probability between now and the end of the project.	January 1st (project end)
			The two sides have agreed on the BetAlpha name and brand. Finalizing through legal.	1 Month

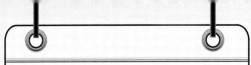

Appendix **B**

Risk Management in the ISO Context

ISO 31000 - Risk management

Risks affecting organizations can have consequences in terms of economic performance and professional reputation, as well as environmental, safety, and societal outcomes. Therefore, managing risk effectively helps organizations to perform well in an environment full of uncertainty.

ISO 31000:2009, *Risk management – Principles and guidelines*, provides principles, a framework, and a process for managing risk. It can be used by any organization regardless of its size, activity, or sector. Using ISO 31000 can help organizations increase the likelihood of achieving objectives, improve the identification of opportunities and threats, and effectively allocate and use resources for risk treatment.

However, ISO 31000 cannot be used for certification purposes, but does provide guidance for internal or external audit programs. Organizations using it can compare their risk management practices with an internationally recognized benchmark, providing sound principles for effective management and corporate governance.

Related Standards

A number of other standards also relate to risk management.

ISO Guide 73:2009, Risk management – Vocabulary complements ISO 31000 by providing a collection of terms and definitions *relating* to the management of risk.

ISO/IEC 31010:2009, Risk management – Risk assessment techniques focuses on risk assessment. Risk assessment helps decision makers understand the risks that could affect the achievement of objectives as well as the adequacy of the controls already in place. ISO/IEC 31010:2009 focuses on risk assessment concepts, processes and the selection of risk assessment techniques.

PMI Risk Management Professional

(PMI-RMP)

PMI's Risk Management Professional (PMI-RMP®) credential is a globally recognized certification specialist role in project risk management.

It recognizes expertise and competency in assessing and identifying project risks, mitigating threats, and capitalizing on opportunities, while still possessing a baseline knowledge and practical application in all areas of project management.

pmi.org/certifications

Glossary

Acceptance – A risk strategy that involves a lack of action related to the risk event prior to the event's occurrence. *See also Passive Acceptance and Active Acceptance*

Active Acceptance – A risk strategy that involves no proactive measures to be taken, but does incorporate outlining the reactions that will occur should the risk event come to pass.

Affinity Diagram – A diagram created by grouping similar ideas into common groups without pre-ordained categories. The categories are labeled only after all ideas with common affinities are grouped.

Avoidance – A threat strategy where the risk event can no longer have an impact on the objective. Avoidance is often accomplished by eliminating the approach to the objective or eliminating the objective altogether.

Audit – *See Risk Audit and Risk Management Plan Audit.*

Beta Distribution – A plot of data points in a graph with a tendency (more data points) toward either the higher or lower end of the scale.

Brainstorming – Idea generation in a group setting where the effort to generate ideas continues until all ideas are exhausted. Conducted without criticism or critique.

Brainwriting – A specific type of written brainstorming that involves writing down ideas, sharing them among peers, and generating a fixed number of answers to a given concept.

Category – A breakdown of risk into like types, normally associated with the source(s) of the risk event(s).

Cause and Effect Diagram – Also known as a Fishbone Diagram or an Ishikawa Diagram. A branched diagram that allows for the display of multiple common causes towards a single effect. May be developed using the "Five Whys."

Contingency Plan – Also known as a Contingent Response. A reactive plan to respond to risks if or when they occur.

Contingency Reserve – Funds or time set aside at a project or departmental level to contend with risks within departmental or project purview.

Contingent Response – *See Contingency Plan.*

Delphi Technique – An anonymous idea-generation technique conducted in iterations to achieve the consensus of experts (often in remote locations).

Detectability – A criterion used in Failure Mode Effect Analysis to highlight the relative ability of the risk owner to perceive the occurrence of the risk event prior to, or during, its occurrence.

Distribution – In statistical analyses, the plotting of data points in a graph to display the relative number of outcomes associated with iterative trials. *See also Normal Distribution, Beta Distribution, Triangular Distribution, and Uniform Distribution.*

Enhancement – An opportunity response strategy that involves efforts to increase the probability or impact or both of the opportunity event.

Event – The episode or incident that may or may not happen in an environment of uncertainty.

Expected Monetary Value – A quantitative analysis technique that involves multiplying the value of the impact (in financial, schedule or quality terms) times the probability of the impact.

Expected Value – *See Expected Monetary Value.*

Expiration – The time or situation at which a risk no longer can influence objectives.

Exploitation – An opportunity response strategy that involves ensuring that an opportunity (which remains a probabilistic event) will definitely come to pass in the organization's favor.

Failure Mode Effects Analysis – A quantitative analysis technique that involves identifying a single risk event (failure mode) and the probabilities of the various impacts that may stem from that event.

Fishbone Diagram – *See Cause and Effect Diagram.*

Five Whys – An approach to questioning commonly associated with a Cause and Effect Diagram. The approach consists of repeating the question "Why" at least five times to learn the root causes of problems or risks.

High Impact – The outcome of a risk event that will substantially harm or limit the objectives for the undertaking.

High Probability – The situation where the likelihood of the associated risk event is considered elevated in comparison to other risk events and their likelihood.

Impact – The severity of the outcome that may occur if a risk event happens.

Individual Risk Analysis – The assessment of the level of risk created by a single risk event, either in absolute (money or time) or in terms relative to other risks on the project or in the organization.

Ishikawa Diagram – *See Cause and Effect Diagram.*

Lesson Learned – The mechanism, strategy, approach, technique and/or trick that proved to be helpful or hurtful during the evolution of a risk event. Such lessons are only considered "learned" when shared with the larger organization as a whole.

Likelihood – *See Probability.*

Low Impact – The outcome of a risk event that will have a negligible effect on the objectives for the undertaking.

Low Probability – The situation where the likelihood of the associated risk event is considered infrequent relative to other risks in the organization.

Management Reserve – Funds or time set aside at an executive level to contend with risks outside departmental or project purview.

Mean – The average of data points in a statistical distribution.

Mitigation – A threat response strategy that involves minimizing either the probability of the threat event or the impact or both.

Models – Evaluative tools that incorporate consideration of a variety of different criteria (with weights) to determine the relative levels of risk (both threat and opportunity) on a given project or undertaking. Examples include the decision scorecard.

Monte Carlo – An iterative, simulation-based, analysis of project outcomes that generates a probability curve on the overall likelihood of achieving objectives.

Normal Distribution – In statistical analysis, a plot of data points in a graph where the data points have an even (and declining) frequency the further they are plotted from the mean.

Objective – Specific goal or target that a project, individual or organization is aiming to achieve.

Opportunity – A positive risk event.

Overall Risk – A relative assessment of a risk, taking into account both the probability and impact of the risk event.

Passive Acceptance – A risk strategy that involves no action outside of basic documentation of the risk event.

Priority – The ranking (relative or absolute) of the risk in terms of other risks under consideration.

Probability – The likelihood of an event occurring.

Probability and Impact Matrix (PxI Matrix) – A spreadsheet or graphic view with Probability on the y axis and Impact on the x axis used to highlight those risks (evaluated qualitatively) in the higher zones (High-probability, High impact and Medium probability, High impact).

Program Evaluation and Review Technique (PERT) – An estimate that sums the best-and worst-case scenario and four times the most likely scenario and then divides by six to provide a mean outcome for the scenario in question. *See also Three-point Estimate.*

Pugh Matrix – A spreadsheet view that displays multiple risk events on one axis and multiple strategies on another axis to highlight the risk response strategies that are most effective at dealing with the risk events.

Qualitative Risk Analysis – The process of prioritizing risks for further analysis or action by assessing and combining their probability of occurrence and impact.

Quantitative Risk Analysis – The process of numerically analyzing the effect of identified risks on overall project objectives.

Reassessment – The reevaluation of any or all elements of the risk management process to determine if there is a change in the existing state. Used to cycle back to the appropriate step of the risk management process and take appropriate action. Generally conducted when change is planned, change occurs, and/or at regular intervals.

Response – The activity, deliverable or process by which an individual risk will be managed.

Register – *See Risk Register.*

Reserves – Money or time set aside to deal with risks. May be used with a modifier, such as management reserve, contingency reserve.

Retirement – *See Risk Retirement.*

Risk – The events, with varying degrees of uncertainty that may have a positive or negative influence on project or organizational objectives. Also, the event, probability and amount at stake associated with any given risk.

Risk Analysis – *See Whole-project risk analysis or Individual-risk analysis.*

Risk Attitude – The belief system or risk perspective of an organization or the preponderance of the organization's members. A chosen position on risk.

Risk Audit – A planned, coordinated review of the efficacy of risk plans and planning and the outcomes of those plans and planning. *See also Risk Management Plan Audit.*

Risk Breakdown Structure – A decomposition of the risks in a hierarchical structure, arranged by their sources.

Risk Categories – Organized groupings of risks by like topics or natural affinities.

Risk Community – Any group of individuals contending with common risks or individuals serving a common objective and contending with the risks associated with that objective.

Risk Culture – The normalized behaviors (or lack thereof) within an organization that represent the degrees of risk tolerance, risk aversion, and risk acceptance deemed acceptable.

Risk Expiration – *See Expiration.*

Risk Finances – The investments made to deal with risks.

Risk Management – The practice of dealing with risks in a process-oriented fashion to keep risks within organizational tolerances.

Risk Management Plan – A document outlining the details of risk management approaches, terms, tolerances, timing, and process.

Risk Management Plan Audit – A planned, coordinated review of the implementation of the risk management plan to determine its efficacy in ensuring consistent risk practice. *See also Risk Audit.*

Risk Manager – An individual with responsibility for overseeing the risk management process.

Risk Owner – An individual with responsibility for overseeing and being accountable for a given risk event.

Risk Priority Number (RPN) – The expense of the event, the probability of the event occurring, and its detection (probability that the event would be detected before the user was aware of it).

Risk Register – Spreadsheet or document providing information about individual risks and their strategies, including event, probability, impact, response, owner, and review date(s).

Risk Response – The action or reaction to the risk to improve the posture of the organization in terms of the impact of the risk on objectives.

Risk Retirement – The managerial act of removing a risk from the risk register for future consideration because it has expired and can no longer influence the objective.

Risk Strategy – *See Risk Response.*

Risk Strategy Matrix – *See Pugh Matrix.*

Risk Triad – The event, probability, and amount at stake associated with any given risk event.

S-Curve – A graphic display of costs or work planned or incurred over time.

Severity – *See Impact.*

Sharing – An opportunity response strategy that involves efforts to increase the probability of an opportunity event by shifting some of the risk to a third party.

Strategy – *See Risk Response.*

SWOT – A four-square graphic analysis that highlights organizational strengths and weaknesses and highlights them in concert with the opportunities and threats created by a specific effort or project.

Threat – A negative risk event.

Three-point Estimate – An estimate that takes into account the best-case scenario, the worst-case scenario and the most likely outcome. Often used in tandem with the Program Evaluation and Review Technique.

Threshold – A point at which behavior should change as a risk is either occurring or is imminent.

Tolerance – Organizational or project-level or individual limit beyond which risk events become wholly unacceptable.

Tornado Diagram – A horizontal bar graph scaled from highest to lowest degrees of risk influence of individual tasks. This diagram is based on a Monte Carlo analysis.

Transfer – A threat response strategy that involves shifting the burden of a risk, (either in whole or part) to a third party.

Triangular Distribution – In statistical analyses, the plotting of data points in a graph based on three primary data points: the best case, the worst case, and the most likely case.

Trigger – Visible or physical signs indicating that a threshold is being breached or is about to be breached.

Uniform Distribution – In statistical analyses, the plotting of data points in a graph where there is no greater likelihood of data points on the high end, low end, or middle.

Warning Sign – See *Trigger*.

Whole-project Risk Analysis – An evaluation of the overall risk in a project or undertaking to allow for comparisons with current and past efforts, and to determine the degree of risk the organization may or may not be willing to undertake.

William Edwards Deming – Deming was an American statistician, professor, author, lecturer and consultant. He is perhaps best known for the "Plan-Do-Check-Act" cycle popularly named after him.

INDEX

About the Authors

Carl Pritchard, PMP®, PMI-RMP®, EVP is the principal and founder of Pritchard Management Associates, a Global Registered Education Provider (REP) of the Project Management Institute. Pritchard Management is recognized for energized, entertaining project management, and management training in risk, communications, and planning. He serves on the board of directors of ProjectConnections.com, and is the U.S. Correspondent for the British project management magazine, *Project Manager Today*. He has written numerous books on project and risk management, and can be reached at carl@carlpritchard.com.

Karen Tate, PMP®, MBA, PMI Fellow, is founder of *The Griffin Tate Group, Inc.* (TGTG), a charter Global Registered Education Provider of the Project Management Institute. TGTG provides project management training and consulting for everyone in the organization associated with projects—project managers, project team members, project sponsors, and senior managers. She has more than 25 years of domestic and international experience in project management and is the co-author of numerous books on the subject. Karen served for six years on the Global PMI Board of Directors and is a PMI Fellow, PMI's highest and most prestigious award that is presented to an individual. Karen can be reached at ktate@griffintate.com.

Customize our Memory Joggers

Take any Memory Jogger or pocket guide and apply your company's own corporate brand. Customization allows you to creatively combine the contents of GOAL/QPC products with your own documents and training materials. We can deliver to eBooks or print versions.

A Pocket Guide of Tools for Continuous Improvement and Effective Planning

2nd Edition

PROCESS MANAGEMENT & QUALITY
MEMORY JOGGER.

BMW GROUP
Financial Services

Digital Formats

Most of our Memory Joggers are available as digital eBooks. You can use eBooks on your computers, eReaders and tablets. Purchasing in multiple quantities is an excellent way to train across corporate locations or all in the same meeting room. Visit Amazon. com or iTunes to purchase single editions. Multiple copies are available through MemoryJogger.org.

On-site Training

GOAL/QPC's on-site workshops offer the highest rate of educational retention. Host a training workshop for hands-on practice.

Visit MemoryJogger.org for more information.

Answer Key

1. d, **2.** b, **3.** a, **4.** c, **5.** b, **6.** a, **7.** b, **8.** c, **9.** c, **10.** c

Notes: _____

_____

_____

_____

_____

_____

_____

_____

_____

_____

_____

_____

_____

_____

_____

_____

_____

_____